GW00656241

Rainbows

and

Broken Dreams

Reflections on my walk and work with God
by Jane A Guest

Forward by Fiona Castle

Dearest Faith
love & God bless
Jane
xxx

Dedication

To my two gorgeous Granddaughters Lily-Mae Guest and Ava-Rose Guest enjoy Nanny's story, it's also Granddaddy's story and God's story.

The day you were born I fell in love with you, my two shining lights who are heaven sent to me remember Nanny loves you now and forever. Read this story and watch out for God's amazing love which is just for you. Love family with all your heart. Trust God, he is always faithful and follow 'what would Jesus do' in your days, it has helped me and this is my best advice for a wonderful life. Love Nanny Jane XX

The right of Jane Guest to be identified as the Author of the Work has been asserted by her in accordance with the Copyright, Designs and Patents Act 1988.

Copyright © Jane Guest 2019

Self Published by Jane Guest

Cover Design by Liam Battle

A catalogue record of this book is available from the British Library

Printed and bound in the UK by 4edge Limited, Essex, SS5 4AD

ISBN: 978-1-5272465-9-1

All rights reserved.
No part of this publication may be reproduced, stored in a retrieval system, or transmitted at any time or by any means, electronic, mechanical, photocopying, recording or otherwise without the prior permission of the copyright holder. This book is sold subject to the condition that it shall not by way of trade or otherwise be circulated without the publisher's prior consent in any form of binding or cover other than that in which it is published.

Front Cover: Victoria Falls, Zimbabwe,
known locally as 'The Mist that Thunders'
photo taken by Jane Guest

Acknowledgements

Peter John Guest my husband, you are the best and you have been my soul mate all these years, thank you for a wonderful, exciting life and thanks for always standing by me, I am because you were there. I love you now and forever.

Mum and Dad I love you with all my heart but because you loved and chose me first and adopted me, I shall be eternally grateful love from your daughter.

Thank you Bro's for your love, I love you too, Stephen, Graham and Malcolm.

Thanks to Pete's Mum and Dad for loving me as a daughter and for all your support. Thank you to all my Sister in laws, love you guys and thank you for being "like sisters to me".

Thank you for your help Melanie and Carol for reading and editing my book in the early years. More recently heartfelt thanks Angela Lucas for your wisdom and all your encouragement. Thank you Pete and Trudy for reading my book through too. May God bless you all dear friends.

A huge thank you to Fiona Castle for your time and kind words they made a real difference, God bless you.

Havens Hospices thank you to all the patients both present and past who taught me how to provide spiritual care and for allowing me to walk by your side, my heartfelt thanks. To the staff I loved working with you and knowing you all. May God bless and continue to guide Havens Hospices in to the next exciting chapter.

Grateful thanks to Liam, Lily-mae's Dad, for helping get my book to print.

Thank you to my Lord and my God for calling me to write our story, what a wonderful adventure it has been. I hope you are pleased.

Contents

Foreword

As most of my friends will know, I am a bit of a Cliff Richard fan and in 1998 a friend from church phoned me and asked if I would like to see Cliff Richard in a concert as another friend had dropped out at the last minute. Of course I said yes. It was a wonderful show and Fiona Castle had been Cliff's special guest speaker.

At the interval of the concert I went to phone Peter to tell him that I would be leaving Wembley shortly, as I did this I came face to face with Fiona Castle. There was no-one else around and it felt like a special moment in time. I started saying that it had really helped me hearing her share her stories about her late husband Roy Castle and went on to explain, in brief, my own battle with Cancer. Fiona was very gracious, and she said one thing I shall never forget, "Jane, make sure you become better, not bitter." And that really helped me. I praised God. My heavenly Father knew just what I needed at this time, an all-important word of encouragement.

Foreward by Fiona Castle OBE

"In this 'chance' meeting with Jane at Wembley, I was surprised that such words came out of my mouth! It was not an expression I had used, before or since, but as you will gather from reading Jane's extraordinary account of her life, God does speak in mysterious ways!

This is a poignant and sometimes very painful story of the struggles of a young woman, openly expressed to give others courage to face the darkest times. As she says, she has seen how God has used her most difficult experiences to help others. She gives a blunt and often gut-wrenchingly honest account of her experiences.

May God bless you Jane, and others through you, for having the courage to write this incredible story.

Jim Graham, Pastor and a wonderful man of God, once said, "Don't forget in the darkness, what God has taught you in the light." I added, "and don't forget in the light what God has taught you in the darkness." Jane, by her experience, has definitely learnt this lesson!"
Fiona Castle

Since then so much has changed I am now a Nanny, obviously a Mum and a fully accredited Baptist Minister.

Preface

Nearly two decades ago I believe God gave me a vision to write a book and so I started to write on the 3rd May 2000 and here it is! As I was sharing my plans with my husband and some friends one summer evening, God gave me the title "Rainbows & Broken Dreams". This is therefore the direct result of a sense of calling. I would never presume to think my life as important enough to write a book about, however I do believe that maybe God wants someone to come across it to maybe help them, comfort them or inspire them in their journey. I did try to take the book further nine years ago but it was not to be and the door closed, and now the way is clear, so may God bless this book and as I humbly tell you my story may it be of help to someone and the larger story be told of the faithfulness of a loving God.

Chapter 1: Against all the odds, I made it with God's help!

On a cold day, if I look very closely, I can still see a scar on each bridge of each finger of my hands, these were the life lines that fed my tiny body and kept me alive as a premature baby, as I lay in my incubator, I weighed 2lb, 14 oz. I was three months premature and fighting for my life. I know now with great assurance that God's hand has been on my life from the very beginning, I can see it as clear as day and I am grateful. So my first home initially was a general hospital in the heart of England, Gloucestershire and with care and attention I survived. I was then moved to London, to the Thomas Coram Foundation for Children, a children's home, an orphanage in the heart of London, which is still doing a fantastic job caring for children and giving essential hope and help, God bless them. My birth mother had given me up for adoption as she was at the tender age of sixteen when I was born. I will always be grateful to my birth Mum that she went through with the pregnancy and birth.

My third home was to be a foster home, but this was to be a short visit, as I was indeed a cry baby and the foster parents could not cope with me and so back I went to Thomas Coram and waited. Understandably, I was a small insecure baby who, must have, felt the bond of my birth Mother's absence keenly. But God's provision for me was soon to come my way, in the form of Mr Walter Len Kerly and Mrs Sylvia Kerly who came to the home and chose me and took me home with them, for which I will always be eternally grateful for all the love and sacrifice from the tender age of 6 months of age. My Mum was an experienced Mum of two boys, my two new brothers and knew just what to do and my mum has an exceptional love of babies, just what I had great need of. My Mum tells me, she used to wrap me tightly in a shawl and lay me in my crib and I was fine. As a result of that love and security of my new Mum and Dad I was one contented little baby.

At the age of seven or so, my Mum and Dad explained, carefully that I was special to them and that when I was a baby they had not had me themselves but had, in fact, chosen me to be adopted, as they were unable to have a little girl and that they had picked me out to be their only daughter. By this time I had three lovely brothers, Stephen, Graham and Malcolm and a great Mum and Dad who I adored and we are close as if we had been blood related to this day.

A wonderful Psalm, and may have well been written by King David, King of Israel, around 1000 BC, I have often reflected in wonder at it, Psalm 139;

> For you created my inmost being; you knit me together in my mother's womb. I praise you because I am fearfully and wonderfully made; your works are wonderful. I know that full well. My frame was not hidden from you when I was made in the secret place. When I was woven together in the depths of the earth; your eyes saw my unformed body. All the days ordained for me were written in your book before one of them came to be.[12]

There is a sense of purpose and that God sees all and knows all and even greater than that he has a plan for your entire life, so comforting that our heavenly Father

---

[1] *Footnote: Psalm 139.13-16,Oxford NIV Scofield Study Bible, ed C I Scofield (Oxford: University Press, 1964)*

[2] *Footnote: "Seventy-three psalms bear David's name – some, no doubt, dedicated to him as king; some collected by him; and a good many surely, his own composition.": p329,* The Lion Handbook to the Bible *(Lion Publishing, 1988)*

used a King to write such tender words and for all generations to draw comfort from.

One day Mum was in the garden at Whitmore Way, Basildon and noticed the lady, living opposite us and recognised her as a friend from long ago. It turned out that they had worked together in London when they were young girls but had lost contact. This faithful Christian lady, Eileen Taylor and her family were to become influential in my life and my finding faith in Jesus Christ. A renewed friendship was struck up and Mum would take me round to see Eileen who was expecting her own baby. The baby arrived, Caroline, and from then till now we are great best friends.

I was walking back from school one day with Mum and Caroline and I remember so clearly that Caroline asked my Mum if I could go to Sunday school with her that week. I remember vividly thinking I don't want to go, don't make me go, please say "No" Mum, all this was going on in my head and then I heard my Mum say "Yes", of course, and my heart sank. I believe now that just at the tender age of five there can be an inward struggle, a wishing to do what you want, a struggle for independence and dare I describe a rebellion in my heart towards God, well there was in mine.

I went that Sunday and had a great time at church, then and every other Sunday thereafter, with Uncle Len, Caroline's Father, who would faithfully pick me up in his car and drive us each week. Then on Sunday evenings I went round Caroline's for tea, I still have a love of Marmite on toast and Birds trifle. We had great times of fun together, playing dolls, board games, jacks and making recordings and playing out and I remember reciting "The Lord's my Shepherd" to Auntie Eileen and learning it by heart.

At the age of eleven, I attended summer camp near Lowestoft, where I gave my life to the Lord Jesus Christ, I remember I knelt down in a tent with the youth leader, a lovely young woman and prayed asking Jesus to come in to my life and forgive me my sin. I remember feeling so happy and full of joy for the rest of the holiday. On returning from the holiday, I remember sitting on the stairs waiting to tell Mum about my prayer, feeling nervous. But I did it and at the age of fourteen both Caroline and I desired to be baptised by total immersion, being baptised, just like the Lord Jesus was, it was great, our families came and watched us and heard our testimony's of faith. Ingaway Chapel, Lee Chapel South in Basildon gave me such a good grounding in biblical knowledge through my early years and teen years, these were happy days. There was a large youth group and we had great teachers. Ingaway Chapel, now Ingaway Church have invited me regularly over the years to preach which has been a total joy to me. Caroline and John her husband have supported me by coming to my early preaching appointments, believing in my calling and helping me with some financial support through my Theology degree, so grateful to God for you both.

Chapter 2: My dream and then… My way

All I ever wanted was to work in a bank in London. I still remember clearly, I was just sixteen when I had an entrance exam for Nat West Bank, and my dear Dad came with me for moral support. I was successful and all this happened before my having taken my final school year exams, I was so happy. It was a dream come true.

I started work in the bank in June 1980, I remember thinking how I loved the work and that I even got paid for it. There were about eighty young people all starting work at the same time, at the Clearing Bank, in Alie Street, Aldgate. We spent our days, sorting rejected cheques by hand in the morning, chatting together and then reconciling computer print outs with the cheques in the afternoons. We had two restaurants, where we had a twenty minute tea break morning and afternoon and a hour lunch break, a monthly disco and even a long bar, over three thousand people worked there, it was an amazing time.   I then went on the work in Quality Control and the IT Departments, I had a ball, and it was such fun. I was earning an excellent wage and could afford to go on holidays abroad and drive my own car. Having said all of this, most of all I owe the bank a lot, as I grew up there I developed confidence and a self-worth the insecurities of my young school days were long gone now. I made friends for life, dearest Jan Frith, rest in peace dearest friend till we meet then forever, Jan was like a sister to me. Dear Sue Smith, both giving me the honour to be God Mum to their boys Daniel and Alex. Mentioning and including here my God Son Benjamin from childhood special friend Lorraine.

But then I did start living totally for myself, what I wanted I could have, I still went to church but now I had a boyfriend, all the friends and clothes I could dream of and holidays abroad. I often felt torn in my relationship and in my love for God. After some time we parted ways, it was heart breaking, but with help from family and a dear friend I got through. Thanks Stephen and Elaine for your love and support not just at this time, but throughout my whole life and for giving me two beautiful nieces to love, Lisa and Joanne.

If you can and you do have a strong faith in God, seek and pray and wait for a life partner who shares your faith. It is said, "what doesn't kill you, makes you stronger" I don't like this saying but I have to admit that I grew up quickly and it gave me understanding and empathy.

I believe all people are made in God's image Genesis 1.26 "Let us make man in our image, in our likeness..."

the word for man can be generic and stands for mankind,[3][4] and that God loves all people, "For God so loved the world that he gave his only begotten Son, that whoever believes in him shall not perish but have eternal life."[5] I have seen that there is great creativity, and beauty in every living soul and wonderful potential, but I think when you have a strong faith it is easier to be on the same page with a spouse who also believes, then life can be as easy as breathing as you go forward into the rest of your lives with God together. Pete and I chose to wear Russian wedding rings, each band standing for me, Pete and God.

At the age of nearly twenty one I moved out of home to live in lodgings with a friend's Mum and Dad, we had lots of fun times and I will always remember their kindness and be grateful to them.

[3] *Footnote: English Standard Version, Holy bible, Genesis 1.26*

[4] *Footnote: Holy Bible, ESV, see 5 g (Crossway Publishing, China 2007)*

[5] *Footnote: NIV Bible John 3.16*

Chapter 3: Life Changing Flu

At the age of 23, I was having a bout of flu and resting up in bed. I remember as I started to recover God spoke to me very clearly through a friend, my prayer partner Brenda. She came to see me and said that God had given her a picture of me and my new car and in this picture there was a great big chain attaching me to the car. I knew immediately God was speaking to me about the car, I loved my car I would get in and smile to myself about my little red fiesta. By the end of this week, I was feeling better and went for a walk around the block and said to God "I love that car but if you want me to give it up I will". This was difficult for me, but I knew I had to sell it. I knew it was holding me back, I had accumulated lots of credit card debts, plus I was paying my huge car loan off each month and I just could not get straight financially, with the holidays aboard and all the new clothes. The problem was so bad that I actually had been getting up at 4am in the morning to undertake overtime at the bank and I still did not have enough to sort the problem out and the debt was giving me sleepless nights, it was awful and so I knew in my heart that the car had to go. I said to God "I will put the car in the paper for one week and if the car has not been sold by the end of the week I will take it to mean that I can keep it". The week passed and on the very last day, just as I was thinking that I could keep the car, a young girl came round with her brother, paid me and took my little car away with them, I was amazed!

With the money, I was able to pay off the car loan and pay off all my debts too, which meant that I could now get up at a reasonable hour in the morning for work. God knew what was best.

Whilst working one day I looked up over my desk to my colleague and friend Sue and I said, "I'm not going to be working here much longer," Sue said "why where are you going?" I replied, "I don't know I just have a feeling that I will not be here much longer". One year later, almost to the day, I left Nat West Bank after eight and a half years, God was moving me on.

Chapter 4: Church Work

At eighteen I had started attending Basildon United
Reformed Church, Honey pot lane, Basildon. When I
was twenty four, the church were considering taking on
a church worker and I felt compelled to apply. The post
paid for lodgings and food. The most wonderful thing
happened, my friend Sue from Nat West said when I
explained about the church work that she would be
happy to sponsor me ten pound per month to help with
finance, well gradually as I mentioned this to all my
friends and family and they all sponsored me ten pound
per month and I did not ask any of them to. I had the
grand sum of one hundred and fifty pounds a month
coming in to my account through standing orders, may
God bless each one who gave to me at that time and
bless you Sue for such a beautiful thought.

God works in mysterious ways and I'm always saying it.
Every life is unique and every journey on this earth
matters to God. "God loves all he has made" my
paraphrase based on Psalm 145.8-9, I love the impact of
the all inclusiveness of God's love. It is not just my
journey that he has impacted, is impacting and will
continue to impact, but your journey and life too. I
believe and have seen how God blesses all souls in their
journeying through this life, how good triumphs over

evil, evil may seek to rob and take away hope but God longs to intervene and how He is always just a prayer away or a chat away in every situation. I believe simply that there is an A plan and a B plan for each life, for the best all we need to do is put our hand in the hand of God our maker and go that way. I am not saying Christians have an easy life and the truth is life can be messy at times, but it's never boring and it's a wonderful adventure, with such blessings along the way. I am grateful that I was able to stay walking with God for most of my life. Thank you God. I have also seen that there is always another bite of the cherry, God will always use us, no matter our age if we are only willing, it's good news.

The work at the church was slow; we started a coffee bar up called "The Honey Pot", offering a coffee and a chat to anyone wishing to call in the church. I had a team of volunteers and I would say that in the course of the year we had about a hundred people come through the doors and so I believe that it was worth it for that. But the Lord had yet another plan, during the year I felt the Lord speak to me about starting up a Mum & Tot's group; we were given a grant, shortly after the idea came, from Basildon Council to commission a wooden Wendy house with furniture for the children. The group soon expanded and there were soon sixty mums and tots in the church, it was bustling and alive it was great fun. Young, often lonely mum's came week after week into the church and found fun and friendship. This work has continued for thirty years now, wow. Whilst out preaching, one Sunday morning, at Laindon free Church, my good friend, Revd Mike Barrett's Church, a woman afterwards came up to me and asked if I had been at the URC toddler group. She began to explain that at the time she had been fostering children and that she was isolated and had been finding things difficult and how the toddler group had helped her so much. Praise be to God. Often we never know or hear how people are helped and what a blessing this was to hear.

During my year, my minister moved on and so I undertook a lot of pastoral visiting, it was a huge undertaking and training ground for me, it was not easy, in fact I felt ill prepared, but God got me through and I saw God at work. A friend Harriet and church leader at the church was working in London at the time and gave me her car to use by day and with my friends financial support I knew God's provision for me. During the year I went along, with the church to Spring Harvest, a Christian holiday which hires out Butlin's and it was during this time I felt a call to go to Bible College. I remember the speaker talking about Dame Cecily Saunders along the lines that she had been called to be a Nurse and said "No" to her Lord, and felt she couldn't but she then proceeded and then God called her to become a Doctor and again she said "No Lord, I couldn't" but she proceeded again and then God called her to start the Modern Hospice Movement and Dr Cecily Saunders said the same again but she proceeded and God did it, Wow! This word of testimony spoke straight to my heart, it gave me a hope and I knew that 'I couldn't do college, but knew that with God I could and I went up the front for prayer in front of a congregation of hundreds. The impossible was happening I had never been to college and my grades at school had been pretty basic.

My minister, Revd Richard Davis, was praying for me and he said:

> "I have been with you my child, from the very
> beginning,
> All that you have been through has been for a
> reason.
> I love you loving me and I love you very much.
> I have something special for you to do,
> You will lead many people to me.
> Do not be afraid of the tears they are a gift from
> me."

Furthermore he said, "Treasure those words, they were not my words but God's". I knew this because I felt like I was walking on air for the next two days and I was praising God and so happy.

Jesus said, "With man this is impossible, but with God all things are possible."[6] I had a wonderful boost to my faith and I believed in my heart that God would use me in my life.

God is truly great and I ended up more recently giving an annual lecture, for six years, at the London based Baptist College, Spurgeon's College, set up by Charles H Spurgeon himself. The lecture was on Chaplaincy and Spirituality, what a thrill and such fun I had, sincerely thank you Lord. A few years ago, after my lecture, I knew that the Hospice set up by Dame Cecily wasn't far away. So I seized the moment and popped in and visited the Chaplain at St Christopher's, Sydenham and had a quick tour around, it is an inspiring hospice and there was a real sense of life, light and hope there and a sense of the history of touching thousands of lives. All Glory to God!

[6] Footnote: NIV Bible, Gideons, Matthew 19.26

Chapter 5: The Birmingham Bible Institute

The interview date arrived and my dear friend Lorraine offered to come along with me for moral support. We made Birmingham in good time and in fact had time to go into the City Centre after negotiating the notorious spaghetti junction. We parked in the NCP car park and went for a coffee. Then we decided to leave for the college and to our alarm we found that they were several NCP car parks and completely did not know where we had parked our car. So much so I had to phone the college and explain and we ended up being late for my interview. Laughing out loud now, but not at the time. We got there I had the interview and got in to College and I was so happy.

Again friends and family would help me out with the fees, plus I would go temping as a secretary in London for Brook Street Agency in the breaks. I worked hard studying, going to lectures and doing evangelism and chores. At the time, I was not interested in anything else, I was single minded and I even managed to make being Head Girl. Having never accomplished much at school, this was an amazing new experience for me, completing and passing exams and essays over sixty in all.

I met Peter at college and we became friends and both started Birmingham Bible Institute in January 1989. As Peter lived in Wickford and I lived five miles away in Basildon we would travel backwards and forwards together as Pete had a car. Peter and I had to go all the way to Birmingham to meet one another; God does truly work in the mysterious ways.

Mr Bonsall had a reputation when it came to prayers. He was the founder of the BBI and when he prayed for you, you needed to watch out, as we all felt as students, as God listened to Mr Bonsall and there would be a definite result to his prayers. Reverend Henry Brash Bonsall prayed for Peter and I, for you see Peter had started to have feelings for me and he was not happy about it, as he felt he had come to BBI to study the Bible and not have a relationship. However, God apparently had other plans; the college did have a little bit of a reputation for being known by the students as the "Birmingham Bridal College"! Peter went to Mr Bonsall and asked him to pray about the situation, un-be-known to me at this stage. Mr Bonsall had already prayed for me after I had preached a sermon at mid-morning service, praying *"Lord... someone to love her dearly"*. What chance did we have with Mr Bonsall praying for us. This man was a true man of God and a privilege to have known, this side of eternity. Mr Bonsall felt a call from God to start up a Bible College in the UK, whilst living with his mother in the prairies of Canada, he was Canadian and gave up everything to come over to England. Praise God.

I remember Peter telling me how he felt for me during a walk in one of our summer breaks, we had become good friends travelling backwards and forwards to Essex, but I did not have any romantic feelings and I told him so. On our return to BBI one night I had a dream, Peter and I were there together and somehow after that dream my feelings for Pete changed and I was soon to fall head over heels in love with my Peter. It was like a miracle, my heart transformed.

Peter and I started to go out together but we kept it quiet until August 1989, during a half term break Peter and I had got up early to pray one morning and we hadn't been going out very long. It was a special prayer time, whist praying the word 'Marriage' came into my mind and almost simultaneously, Peter said, "Lord if we are to get married please show us the way." On 26th December 1989 Peter and I got engaged to the amazement of family and friends. That following summer in August, we were married at Honeypot Lane, Basildon, Essex, at the United Reformed Church, by our dear friend Reverend Christopher Briggs.

Chapter 6: Cold Feet

Many young couples experience "cold feet" after making a huge commitment to marry and it happened to me.

Peter and I had become engaged I was so very happy and we had the blessing from both sets of parents and the Reverend Bonsall. However, I started to get scared and started questioning myself. We went to see our good friends and Pastor Roy and Oriel Fellows for pre-marriage counselling, this was a tremendous help, supporting me and Pete with love and patience at this crucial time. I discovered that I felt worried that by marrying Pete I would somehow lose my independence. My dear, soon to be husband, assured me that I would always have the freedom to do just what I wanted and that Peter said, he would never tie me down. He then wrote me a beautiful song which included these sentiments; he would often play this to me on his guitar. How blessed was I.

I remember one particular Sunday when Peter had his first preaching engagement scheduled. Early that morning I went to see him and said that I had cold feet and that I felt scared about getting married. This obviously was a big bomb shell and on a day when Pete had a lot, already on his mind with preaching. Peter said let's pray, he prayed that God would give us a particular sign to put all our jitters to rest. I was giving my testimony at the church and was accompanying Pete with the singing. We both made a big effort to put off our feelings and concentrate on the Church Service at hand, which was not easy to do.

We went back to BBI and prepared. The time came to leave for the service. It was a little evangelical church and here is the sequence of events.

I remember standing on the platform and Peter made some mention of the church and that he had been there before, and how the singing had not been in the right key, he promptly started off playing his guitar completely in the wrong key for the next song himself and I had to rescue him by singing extra loud correctly, bless him! Divine retribution we may never know but it was amusing for me afterwards! I then gave my testimony of becoming a Christian and Peter gave the message. The most significant moment was to arrive shortly after the close of the service. A man approached us and gave us a neatly folded ten pound note for our travel expenses and we thanked him and proceeded to go back to our hostels.

Peter asked me if I would like to go for hot chocolate to a talk about my earlier concerns. As we spoke together over our drinks, I started to feel much better but a strange thing was about to happen. We both went up to pay for our drinks and Pete got out the ten pound note and unfolded it, as he did confetti fell all over the floor. Instinctively we both knelt down and started to collect and clear it up. I remember, it was a dark cobbled floor and the confetti, was the large circular kind, white and pink confetti the type that's safe for birds to eat. I picked a handful up and handed it over to Pete and he put it straight in his trouser pocket and he did the same with his handful in his other pocket. I thought how strange and perhaps someone had got married and the money had been the payment for the use of the church. Then when we got into the car, we both started to talk about it, saying things like "do you think that was a sign from God encouraging us about our marriage?" We were quite excited and both feeling in better spirits on our way back to college. We got out of the car and as we were still talking about the strange occurrence, then Pete went to get the confetti out of his pocket and there was none there, not one piece to be found anywhere in fact, his pockets were both completely empty! It was a miracle, plain and simple and we could not believe our eyes, we had both witnessed the event and believe, to this day that it was a miracle from God. After I went in to my hostel, Pete apparently searched the car from top to bottom in search of the confetti but there was no trace of any of it, we both took this to be a tangible answer to Pete's prayer and I seemed to have my mind put to rest from then on.

Chapter 7: The Vision

A day of prayer and fasting for the students and staff would be organised every term at College. An outside speaker would come and talk and we would all be encouraged to retreat and pray. On this particular day, Peter and I decided to go over to Sutton Coldfield Park, it was one of our favourite places to go to. It is a vast park with beautiful wood lands and spectacular views.

I remember Peter saying that he would really like to hear from God in a particular way and so we prayed and fasted asking God to speak to us, during the whole day we prayed and fasted and struggled with the hunger pains and once nearly gave way, but we pushed on through the temptation. During this day, we had times of waiting on God, and Peter had a picture, a type of vision given to him. Peter told no one about the picture for a couple of days, then he told his room-mate and instantly Peter understood what the whole picture meant!

The vision; "A black man was standing at the end of a giant hammer head and the hammer head was as wide as the man was tall and the giant handle of the hammer was laying separate. Then the hammer handle and hammer head came together and was in a giant hand in the sky, and then the hand and hammer came smashing down on to a two storey hut." The interpretation, was an event that would take place, it was in Africa, the meaning came to Pete, "the hammer separated represented Jane and me not married, but when we were married the hammer joined and came together in God's hand, and this represented us being used by God in Africa." No wonder Pete didn't tell me straight away about a possible mission to Africa!

We were to be used by God in a far off land. We held this vision in the back of our minds and now, in the fullness of time, the vision was fulfilled with our calling to Zambia, praise God for his faithfulness to us. God is so good and we have found that life with God is an adventure and he has so much to bless us with in our lives, if we are willing to follow Him. We will never know the extent of how we were used in Chengelo Secondary School, but God ordained that mission, Praise God.

Chapter 8: The Wedding

I had been working in London till the day before my
wedding and as I woke up I immediately looked out of
the window, eager to know the weather forecast for the
day, as today was to be my wedding day 18th August
1990. It had rained in the night, but had been a roasting
hot summer whereby all the grass was now brown.

Rainbows are important to me, I will always strain to
see them, eager to find the beginning and the end
where possible and enjoy all the colours. It was planned
that my bridesmaids would be the colours of the
rainbow, as I had six bridesmaids I chose the colours
pink, yellow, green, blue, peach, lilac, and each
bridesmaid could choose their favourite colour. I also
had three pageboys dressed as sailor boys. The
wedding party all got ready at the same address and it
was such fun. Thanks to friends Shirley and Heather for
making the bridesmaids outfits, they were beautiful,
thank you for all your kindness. Our wedding day, was
one of the best days of my life, it was a big affair, two
hundred people had been invited for the wedding
breakfast, which included family, extended relations
and all our friends from the Bank, Bible College and
some Samaritans friends from when I volunteered.

The Church was packed and it was a beautiful service. I remember feeling nervous as I got into the wedding car, but I felt amazing and dear Dad was right by my side. The dress was chosen with my Mum and Mum in law, the dress I had imagined in my mind had not worked out in reality but the moment I put on "the one" I just knew and both mum's said "that's the one!". It was white, full length, with long sleeves, puffing out to the shoulders in a Princess Diana style and neck line. The dress was fitted to the knees then fanned out into a fish tail train at the back with numerous layers of skirting and netting also pushing out at the front. The veil was short, trimmed in satin, to just below the shoulders and the head dress was a "v" shape of pearls which was positioned forward and I wore my hair up in a French plait, I felt a million dollars.

Before purchasing the dress, I remember coming home and my Dad asked me whether or not I had found a dress, I said that I had, but that it was far too much money. I remember telling Dad the price and how he said, "go ahead and get the dress", my sweet Dad, thank you dear Dad for my dream dress, you made me very happy that day. My dreams and rainbows were all coming together.

Three O'clock came and I walked into the Church holding my Dad's arm to the Hymn "Jesus joy of man's desire" tune by Handel (the composer), it was wonderful. The Church looked great, full of flowers thanks to Pete's Mum and Dad. Our friend Christopher soon put us at ease and took a lovely service for us and a friend from College sung Graham Kendrick's *"Beauty for Brokenness"*. Peter looked very handsome in his Yves Saint Laurent, charcoal pinned striped suit, which his Mum and Dad and Sisters had bought for him. We sung "At the Name of Jesus" and "Great is thy faithfulness". We said our vows facing each other then Pete and I took Holy Communion from the Moderator Revd Keith Bygraves. I was so happy to be Mrs Jane Guest, it was a dream to be married to Pete, my soul mate and for us to share this special moment before our God and with all our loved ones was such an amazing blessing.

The reception was awesome and my dear Mum and Dad, Mother in law and Father in law did so well with giving me another dream come true. As I explained earlier we had two hundred sit down and each table had been set out with different shades of the rainbow serviettes, the flowers were carnations and roses, all the beautiful matching shades of the rainbow. We sat down to a lavish four course meal, after which we had all the speeches, with me giving a word or two too!

Seriously can't ever be stopped, can I. At the evening buffet we had an extra fifty guests, and we had a great DJ and had so much fun dancing and chatting the night away. It was perfect. That is now twenty-nine years ago and I'll always be eternally grateful Mums and Dads, that was just a perfect wedding.

Years later, I got in touch with our photographer from Canvey for some extra wedding prints and she told me how another bride, after seeing my photo's, had copied the colour scheme and styles of the dresses even down to the shape of my headdress, how funny but what a wonderful compliment that was!

Pete's Mum and Dad paid for our honeymoon to the lovely seaside town of Rye, for our two week honeymoon, which was lovely, with my handsome husband.

Chapter 9: Being Homeless

On our return to the South East from living in Birmingham for College for two years, we were aged thirty four and twenty seven and Pete's sister Sally kindly put us up for seven months. We did not wish to outstay our welcome and so Peter and I packed everything up in the car and thought that we would rent somewhere temporarily as we were both working. The unfortunate thing was that we did not realise that we needed at least a thousand pounds deposit for private rental, which we did not have. In fact, we were still paying off some debts accumulated for living expenses whilst at College, which totalled eighteen hundred pounds. On returning to Sally's home we worked hard and paid off the amount by the time we went to pick up our Diploma's at our Valedictory Service in the summer of 1991.

We were both feeling very stressed and did not know which way to turn. Some years previously, Pete had put his name on the council housing list but he was not anywhere close to obtaining any accommodation. We left the council office as night time was approaching and we still had to find accommodation. It was mid-week and we said that we would check in at the local Travel Inn, but when we arrived, they were fully booked, we could hardly believe it, we were shocked and felt a bit like Mary and Joseph with no room at the Inn! The council had actually said that if we were to split up, as a couple and went into separate lodgings this would enhance our chances and priority of getting a flat. This horrified us and there was absolutely no way that we were ever going to split up for anything.

We stayed at Pete's parents for the night and we decided to view some properties to buy but our minds were in a total whirl, we did not have any peace as we went from flat to flat looking for somewhere to live. It was exhausting we just kept on praying for help and guidance. On our return to our parents' home, we were told there had been a phone call from the council who said that they had a flat for us. We could not believe our ears and without delay we went to see the council and quickly got the keys. But when we had visited the flat it was in an awful state and I remember crying when having to sign the tenancy agreement, but I did it.

To give some insight to our flat the locals had a nickname for the housing estate and it was Alcatraz and was built in the 1970's, the block where we lived no longer exists for the local council knocked our part down because it was so unpopular, not surprisingly. The flat was smelly and dreary and all ceilings were stained with yellow cigarette smoke. The council had said that due to the poor state of the flat they would give us six weeks free rent to fund our redecorating. Both of our families were so kind and rallied round which resulted in the whole flat having been cleaned and decorated in one weekend. What a transformation, it had become a beautiful flat and was very spacious with two bedrooms and what I had not paid much notice to before, was a fifteen foot by ten foot balcony area which overlooked some old blossom trees from our second storey. Laindon Link was our first proper home together and Peter and I celebrated our first wedding anniversary there after we moved in on the 1st August 1991, Praise God.

Some five years later due to the council wanting to upgrade the area, the local authority offered us thirteen thousand pound to move out and buy a property of our own, how amazing was that. In the end and due to my ill health we could not commit ourselves to this and they gave us a goodwill cheque of the princely sum of two thousand, five hundred pounds for simply moving on. I calculated that this was the total amount of rent we had paid over five years, wow God is faithful and always seems to work in those mysterious ways. In effect, we had lived there free of charge. What provision could be better!

Chapter 10: The 'Wow' Factor Job

What an experience of a lifetime this job application turned out to be! I'm an ordinary girl, who lived many of her years in the new town of Basildon, but I have an extraordinary God. On our return from Bible College, Pete and I were constantly looking for Christian jobs as we were fresh out of college and we were both very eager to find some purposeful work for God. I saw a job advert for a position as a Youth Pastor working for the Church of Scotland in London and so I applied. I was short listed for an interview by a head hunter. So I prayed and visited the man in his posh house somewhere in the west end of London. I remember being nervous but believed that if it was God's plan I would get the job. The interview was successful and I got through to the next level of the interview process, there were just three of us in the running for the post now.

The next stage of the interview was to visit the church itself for a morning service. It was quite beautiful and spectacular all at once. It happened to be the Church of Scotland, Knightsbridge, just around the corner from Harrods! We drove to the church and as we walked in we simply could not believe our eyes, it was gigantic, with massive stained glass windows letting the light stream down on us, from a very great height, the sun lit up the aisle. The church was reasonably full as I recall, we quietly sat down awestruck. As the church service started, the organ bellowed out its triumphant melodious tones, the vibrations seemed to go right through your body. Then the choir sang, what seemed like, or what I would imagine, angels to sing like in heaven and they were positioned directly behind the congregation and up near to the ceiling, it was an amazing experience. Then there was the procession of Ministers who all walked in their academic robes and clerical collars, their black gowns flowing as they proceeded down the aisle.

One of the ministers took his place in the pulpit, which was large and circular, there was also a high plinth position above him. The scene was set and we enjoyed the service very much.

After the service we were invited to attend lunch which was held in the basement of the church, this was a weekly affair and it was on a large scale, and roast dinner for all. I remember being quite nervous, but I made conversation and kept praying and I made it through. There were just two candidates, myself and one other now. I had my second interview, this time with the other ministers of the church, this I felt went all wrong, perhaps you have known that experience in an interview? I was very sad, but I cheered myself up with a visit to the local corner store and pushed my way through the grand doors of Harrods! Now I was to wait for the phone call. The other applicant I was told lived in the area and had youth work experience and so it turned out that this chap got the job. I was very disappointed, but then it would have meant travelling from Laindon to the West End late at night after youth events and I could see the inconvenience of that and also the safety element. The head hunter was very sorry and said that I had come close. Well in hindsight, I am now grateful that I did not get that job as I would not have gone to Africa and so God, it seemed, had other plans for me. Praise our God he leads and prepares us and shows us the way, we had the experience of a lifetime in Africa, and the Knightsbridge experience was one to never forget too. I thank God for all the rich experiences of life and testify to it being all down to our Almighty God, my Saviour and friend. He is the Creator of true adventures and I give my sincere gratitude and praise for my wonderful life.

Chapter 11: School's Team

Sometimes waiting on God to give you the next thing to do can take a bit of patience, Pete and I experienced that back in Essex and before we went to Zambia. It was during this time that I joined the Basildon Schools Team under the banner of the Basildon Christian Council. With Teacher and Lay Reader Doreen Jennings, Linda Barrett, Angela Lucas, Christine and myself and every term we would take Primary School Assemblies in fourteen schools. It was great fun and we got to know the Heads, Teachers and children all very well, it was a time of blessing. We would use plenty of action Bible based songs, stories, write our own scripts for Bible plays and make all our own props. We would spend our days and time working on new props around Linda's house, we would have a whole lot of fun and laughed a lot I seem to remember. We were received really well and the schools looked forward to our visits. I remember drawing once a three metre Goliath and we would prop it up against the gym scaffold in the school halls and tell the story of David. I remember drawing the temple gate called "Beautiful" to help tell the amazing bible account of healing. [7] The puppet shows

[7] Footnote: NIV Bible, Acts 3.

were many and varied, Linda was excellent at making those and puppetry in general. I remember one line that Linda and Doreen wrote "a sower went to sew, not SEW, SOW" spelling the words out loud!

I remember once I was at a school and my guitar playing was pretty basic and I started the song off in the wrong key and could I get it back on track no but the Head was so helpful and sung extra loud and somehow we made it through. I am sitting here laughing typing this I can remember I got all hot and bothered at the time. Because we were regularly invited back I think we must have done a good job, we certainly poured all our enthusiasm, energy and hearts in to it and enjoyed very much our days of schools ministry.

Chapter 12: Holiday to Israel made the Bible seem to be in Three Dimensions

Pete and I joined some church leaders going to Israel and wow it really brought the Bible to life and seemed to make it ever since be in three dimensions. We arrived by Lake Galilee. I remember we arrived in the evening and it was a warm night and as Pete and I sat by the lake the breeze was like a warm hairdryer blowing into our faces. As we looked across the lake we could see the lights of Capernaum, it was astonishing where Jesus had lived, wow. The next day we went for an early morning swim, which was also amazing. All of the time you are thinking, Jesus was here and the disciples. We went on a boat ride and the winds got gusty and the ministers with us loved it, perhaps they were thinking of the storm when Jesus walked on water to his disciples. When we arrived in Jerusalem, it was incredible, we were looking over at Mount Moriah and the old City and the golden Dome of the Rock, it was an amazing site to see in reality. One afternoon Pete and I decided to do the walk Jesus did from Jerusalem, down the Kidron valley and up to the Mount of Olives. As we walked in the Kidron valley we walked past Absalom's pillar and tomb, King David's son and the tomb of James and the tomb of Zacharias. We also passed the many white stoned tombs in the valley. When we reached the Mount of Olives we ascended the hill and reached the top and looked out over Jerusalem, as Jesus did. It was amazing. However on arrival, there was like a physical tension in the air, I have never experienced it since but there was like a charge of electric in the atmosphere and Pete also felt something. There was an army presence up there and our guide later told us that it could have been dangerous walking in the Kidron Valley but I will never forget it. Pete and I were told off for holding hands on mount Moriah by a Muslim worshipper, at which point we let go of each other immediately.

To have dinner in Jerusalem you never have tea or coffee with milk after your kosher meal as they will not mix the meat and dairy, there truly is nothing like going to a country to experience true culture and geography. We visited the garden of Gethsemane that was very special, we were told that some of the olive trees were in fact two millennia years old, which is very poignant to think they were there possibly when Jesus prayed there. We went to the Church of the Holy Sepulchre said to be the spot where Jesus was buried but it felt very busy and hard to imagine the realities. We went to a tomb near the skull of Golgotha which was said to be of the first century time period and it seemed to give more of an idea and a sense of what the Lord Jesus Christ went through for me and all humankind then and since, it gave me contemplative time. It was like this was the inception place of all that I had believed in for nearly all my life, a pivotal moment, confirming moments of my faith, in this historical ancient City. I love the BC and AD, "Before Christ" and "In the year of the Lord", time lines that we use in our society today, I know Common Era is used too, but mainly the whole of history is based on the time line of Christ, which is amazing to me and I love it.[8]

[8] *Footnote: Wikipedia: The terms anno Domini[note 1][1][2] (AD) and before Christ[note 2][3][4][5] (BC) are used to label or number years in the Julian and Gregorian calendars. The term anno Domini is Medieval Latin and means "in the year of the Lord",[6] but is often presented using "our Lord" instead of "the Lord",[7][8] taken from the full original phrase "anno Domini nostri Jesu Christi", which translates to "in the year of our Lord Jesus Christ".*

This calendar era is based on the traditionally reckoned year of the conception or birth of Jesus of Nazareth, with AD counting years from the start of this epoch, and BC denoting years before the start of the era. There is no year zero in this scheme, so the year AD 1 immediately follows the year 1 BC. This dating system was devised in 525 by Dionysius Exiguus of Scythia Minor, but was not widely used until after 800.[9][10]

The Gregorian calendar is the most widely used calendar in the world today. For decades, it has been the unofficial global standard, adopted in the pragmatic interests of international communication, transportation, and commercial integration, and recognized by international institutions such as the United Nations.[11]

The river Jordan was a beautiful place with its olive coloured waters, it was like nothing I had ever seen. We were able to go into the water and it was special to think that John the Baptist had baptised Jesus, God's Son, somewhere there and he baptised many other followers seeking repentance before God. We visited also the Dead Sea, Golan Heights, and Masada, Bethlehem and Nazareth, we prayed at the Wailing Wall, me at the ladies part and Pete on the men's side. What was astonishing was that Israel is only the size of Wales but there is such varied terrain, from arid desert to lush plantations, to the lowest point on earth, to the mountain of Masada, its an incredible place, truly a land of milk and honey.[9] [10]

Another special place was Jericho and we stood looking over the whole ancient city. At our feet was a water

[9] Footnote 9: NIV, Bible, Genesis 15.18-21& Exodus 3.17

[10] Footnote: Promise of land and fulfilment verses. 'Yahweh promised Abraham that if he followed these laws, he would found a great nation that would live in a land flowing with milk and honey. This land, known as Canaan in ancient times, is roughly located in the same place as modern-day Israel.' www.ushistory.org/civ/4g.asp

cistern that was eight thousand years old we were told. You can see how the City was irrigated and is based around a spring. It is in the desert and all the palms and houses and roads seem to be neatly patch-worked and it seemed like, not much had changed since biblical times. I could imagine the walls of Jericho coming down or Jesus walking around there. It was a very special moment. Thank you Lord.

Chapter 13: Mission to Zambia

I would like to share with you now the events that led up to Peter and I going on mission to Zambia for two years. It all started with our finishing College in January 1991 and coming back to work and live in Essex. We took up regular work and youth work at the URC, Honeypot Lane. This was a wonderful time with the young people and along with many youth weekends at the church, we started up a music group with five young people it was lovely we had two Celloist and guitarist and others we had such fun practicing Spring Harvest songs and introducing them to the church. But we longed for some full time Christian work still.

We sent our C.V's all over the place in the UK, but also to Australia, as Peter had lived there for nine years and had dual citizenship. Then totally out of the blue, for us, one morning we received a letter from Africa, which had attached two application forms, the letter encouraged us to apply to be House parents at Chengelo Secondary School, in Mukusi, Zambia, yes on the continent of Africa. I remember the day the letter arrived and the feeling of total dread that came over me, thinking "the UK yes Lord, Australia yes Lord, but Africa... No Lord!" I had a bike ride to work and remember feeling physically sick on the way due to the thought of it all.   We later found out our two friends who had put our names forward to the school un-be-known to us, were our Pastor from Birmingham, Revd Roy Fellows and Oriel Fellows.

Later as Peter and I were looking at the job application and accompanying letter, we noticed that it said "if you are not totally sure that this job is for you, please do not complete the form" Phew… we both looked at each other and said "fine we won't!" But we did send our C V's off and said "we feel we have nothing to offer you at the school".

Some weeks later, one Sunday morning as we were having a cuppa in bed before church and the phone rang and it was the Head Master Neil Solomon from Chengelo School phoning from Zambia saying "you have everything we need, when can you come?" I said I needed to talk with my husband and could he phone back in an hour. We said "yes" to them and said "if God willed it, we would go." A promise from the Bible:-

> "This is what the Lord says your Redeemer, the Holy One of Israel; I am the Lord your God, who

teaches you what is best for you, who directs you in the way you should go". [11]

At the time we were still living in our council flat and knew that we had to go and see the housing officers, as we would not give up our home, and have no home to come back to. This was our Fleece before God. In the book of Judges, the Bible talks about,[12] Gideon who had asked God for a sign and it was to do with the fleece of a sheep. Peter and I felt sure that if this was of God and His perfect will for our lives, we would be able to keep our flat on somehow and that would confirm to us that this was the will of God.

We visited the Council and explained to the lady that we had been given an opportunity to work for two years voluntarily in Zambia and asked could there be any possibility of keeping our flat on please? She said "well the odds are ninety-five percent against you but write a letter explaining everything anyway". We did and were soon to learn God likes those sort of odds.

[11] Footnote: NIV Bible, Isaiah 48.17

[12] Footnote: NIV Bible, Judges 6.37

We went home and sat down to write our letter explaining to the Council that we had an amazing opportunity to work as House Parents in a boarding school, as missionaries in the middle of Africa and how we needed the opportunity to keep our flat so that after the two year contract ended we would have a home to come back to and we would appreciate it very much if they, the council would consider letting us sublet our flat, until our return. This was a long shot we both knew.

We then carried on as normal working, at the time Peter was working for his Dad, a Grower, in Horticulture, Battlesbridge and I was helping out Sally, Pete's sister selling plants on her market stall in Basildon, for the season.

Neil Solomon the founding Head Teacher at the Secondary School, was expecting us in January 1993. It was now October and Peter and I had not heard back from the Council. Both Peter and I were very keen by now to go to work in Zambia, but we were taking it all in our stride. I needed to phone the Council regarding our flat and we also needed to book our flights to Lusaka, the Capital of Zambia. I remember the day so clearly and remember feeling nervous. I spoke to the housing officer again and explained that we needed to know one way or the other and told her that we would not go if it meant we would be homeless on our return. She said, "Well Mrs Guest, I am pleased to tell you that you can keep your flat on and sublet." I was absolutely shocked, but also very excited. It is a general fact that local councils never normally let tenants sublet their flats. We both felt it was God's confirmation to us that God had worked a mighty miracle and removed a big obstacle in our way of getting to Zambia.

The time was drawing closer and we had many expenses to take care of, or should I say God had, as one thing after another, every single need was met by a miracle. I shall explain, on a visit to our GP we were told that we needed the following vaccinations Hepatitis A, Typhoid, Yellow Fever, Tetanus, Polio and Rabies and we also needed to take the boosters with us for Hepatitis and Rabies. We had to pay for all of these injections as we were not going on a holiday but actually living in the country, the problem being our funds were low. I remember going to Church one Sunday and all we had was our thirty pound offering. Peter said to me, "shall we keep it towards the expense of the injections?" We both decided it should go in to the collection and so it did. That day God truly blessed us. As we were walking out of our church that morning Basildon United Reformed Church, the Minister,

Reverend Martin Kitchener, handed us a cheque for three hundred pound. God had been true to His word. In the Bible, the book of Malachi, 3.10 says, "Bring the whole tithe into the storehouse, that there may be food in my Heaven and I will pour out so much blessing that you will not have room enough for it." We were so encouraged and happy, we had our injections and paid for them all, Praise God.

Now we had to find one thousand and six hundred pounds for the air fares, Christian friends from all over Basildon began to give freely. Every day almost we received cheques and money through the post, and it was truly moving and a very humbling experience. One dear friend Doreen actually sold her car to help us with our air fares to Zambia. The late, Doreen Jennings a faithful friend and a faithful hearted Christian servant to our Lord.

We had just two weeks to go now before our departure and Peter said to me, "unless we sold our car we would still not be going to Zambia", I could not believe he said that, I just knew by this stage that we were going and had actually reached the point of no return and nothing was going to stop us. He said that we could not leave as we needed to pay off the car loan first before leaving the country! This is what happened next, we had put an advertisement in the local paper and on the last evening we received a phone call from a relative of a brother in law, who was desperate for a vehicle and she was interested in our car. She came round the very next day and paid us the asking price in cash which was two thousand and five hundred pounds. Pete and I were on our way and we were both very excited and apprehensive all at the same time, this seems to be the combination of emotions for a life adventure. It was a hard experience saying farewell to family, there were many tears but my Dad had said "go and explore your horizons" and that was his blessing when we had told him and my Mum. Many times in my life, it seems God will move in a situation just at the eleventh hour. He is never too early and never too late, but steps in just at the right time. Our faith now high by all these experiences we knew we could completely trust in our God going to Africa.[13]

[13] *Footnote: Bible reference 11th hour concept, NIV Bible Matthew 20.18-19 Jesus talking about employing people and paying them all the same, even when it is late in the day, Jesus was referring to the saving grace of God which is for all, even those who choose late in the day, you will get the same saving grace as the others who choose* faith earlier. *But God too seems too often work at the 11th hour, in situations, maybe this is a sort of testing our faith.*

We arrived in Africa safely, on our British Airways flight on the 30th January 1993, with a fifty US dollar traveller's cheque in our pocket. We spent two wonderful years of hard work and joyful adventures of living on the continent of Africa. There were challenges but I really felt that God had got us there and then He said come on you two get on with the job now. It is said that once you experience Africa it will always be in your blood, we will never forget our wondrous time there, it changed our perspective on life completely and we have tried to look after the resources God has blessed us with ever since.

One time, whilst we were living there, we had put a chicken carcass on the outside boiler fire and there was a knock on the door, it was one of the locals, a school worker and he asked if he might have the carcass for food for his family.[14] I know that many people today boil up a chicken carcass and that it makes for a good soup, but this was life changing, in that the humility of this man and his need for his family. I know that I have

[14] *Footnote: Both Pete and I have been vegetarian's for twenty five years now.*

tried to live as a good steward of all that God has blessed us with, I know it changed me forever, seeing people living in mud huts with no electricity and hole in the ground toilets. It is said in Africa the cleanest loo is behind a tree and it is true. Remember, some of you going back to the sixties and car travel without service stations and the trip behind the nearest tree? Yes it was like being little again.

We were House Parents to sixty boys aged between eleven and sixteen years and we were also told on our arrival that we would also be Religious Education Teachers. With the support of Roy Fellows our friend, who was also a brilliant Teacher and with his help we managed to introduce the new IGCSE RE syllabus. On our arrival all we had been given for a resource was a box of old exercise books. When we left we left behind ten box files full of resources for the next RE teachers. Praise God what a miracle that was.

What a wonderful time we had at the school, I remember our first weekend we were put on-call duty for the school and had to do regular patrols around the grounds looking after over two hundred pupils. We met, and had, such wonderful, friendship and fellowship with the other teachers and staff. We were all of the same thinking, working ethic and faith and we all lived together in community. Because you are all in it together, living and resting, holidaying there is like a greenhouse effect on your relationships and it made us all, the staff, very close.

Neil Solomon was such a wonderful Headmaster and friend the one and only Neil, a one in a zillion, RIP dear Neil. It was an honour to be teaching there and although it was tough at times and challenged us, it was an unforgettable journey and we trust and pray that we accomplished all that God wanted from us. I remember at six O'clock every night in the hostel, the homesick little lads in year 7, would all queue up, missing their Mums and Dads and would come to us for a bit of reassurance, bless them they were so lovely. When we would be teaching and entered the class room all the pupils would stand and say "Good morning Mrs Guest", it felt like maybe this was like going back in time fifty years in England. I remember one weekend Pete and I had gone to the Moffat's Farm Retreat for a rare night off and when we returned, one of the urinals had broken and sixty pairs of feet had been walking urine all over the hostel and with the heat you can only imagine the smell. Swiftly we dispensed buckets of hot water and gloves and we all went to work cleaning.

I remember one of the hardest things that Pete and I had to undertake was telling a sixth former that his parent had died, this was very sad and hard to do, but because he was one of our young leaders it was felt it was best coming from us. Bless him. We did our best to give comfort and prayed for him. Zambian people are beautifully gentle and laid back in their nature.

Another tale to tell because I liked swimming and had swum a mile for charity in my past, I was put in charge of our Chengelo Swimming Team. Well what can I say, they swam like fish, and some were even swimming for the national team! We had a stunning outside pool, with seating stands surrounding, the pool was often used for baptisms too. .I would march up and down the pool side with my whistle blowing and shouting, "Four lengths front crawl, four breast stroke, four back stroke, four butterfly Go!" The team were amazing swimmers and I could not have been less qualified for the task, but hey ho, it was fun and hopefully I helped.

In Britain there are always lots of people behind you in the queue for any type of work, all qualified and able to the task, not so when you are living in a developing country however. The picture is very different, there are only a few qualified workers and you end up doing all sorts of jobs as a result, it is a nice feeling and I remember covering a Maths lesson one time, which was funny because I did not get my grade C, GCSE Maths till night school sometime later.

In another P.E. lesson I was teaching volleyball on the outside courts, we had about thirty children in our classes and there were about four courts and all was going well. But after a while of standing I became uncomfortable as some red African ants had gone up my tracksuit legs and were biting me. Alarmed and in real pain... I kept my cool and just about said "You, you and you are in charge, I just have to nip back to the hostel" and I legged it back. How funny but painful it actually is to have ants in your pants!

Our tap water was from the local stream and our drinking water from the borehole and both were tinged with a copper red rust colour and I used to joke that you went into the shower cleaner than when we came out. When we did come home we had both lost a lot of weight Pete had a pair of trousers that when done up could fall to the ground. We lived with a constant, uninvited friend called dysentery for most of our time but we had a fabulous nurse, Nurse Ruth and local laboratory that would find out what type of dysentery it was and treated it swiftly.

The cockroaches were everywhere and I remember we would hang our bread up in a bag, on a piece of string at night hoping they would not get in to it. Cockroaches have a unique, awful smell about them, we were getting out our plates on a daily basis and there were always black eggs on them, I think it was the heat. One day I had had enough and I painted inside and outside all my kitchen cupboards and drawers with the necessary chemicals and we let chemical smoke bombs off which eradicated the creatures from all our living spaces and our flat was clean.

My Pete had received a wonderful God given gift whilst we were there for taking whole School Assemblies. I guess it was the gift of parable telling and there was always a moral to the story. The reaction of the whole school was amazing; you could hear a pin drop, when Pete was telling his stories. One time the whole school were at Assembly, two hundred and fifty pupils, and as Pete was announced the whole school started to clap their hands applauding and he hadn't even said a word yet. Here is one talk:

> "There was an American Indian Chief, called
> Running Water and he had three children
> named, Hot, Cold and Luke. There was a boy in
> the village and he liked "Hot" the chief's

daughter. And he thought she was hot! Every night he would lie in bed thinking about her and one night whilst he was lying there, there was a tap at the window and when he looked out who should be standing there but Hot. Then she said "Come outside, I want to have a talk with you" and so he went outside and they walked across to the park and as they were walking she slipped her hand in his and he thought things are looking good. Then they stopped and sat down and she told him that she really liked him and she laid back and said "You can kiss me if you like." And as he rolled over to give her a kiss, he rolled straight off his bed to the floor; the whole thing had been a dream. Don't waste your life living in a fantasy world, get real."

Some years after, one of the South African teachers wrote in a letter saying to Pete "How did you do it? It was a real gift".

Chapter 14: Pete's Story by Pete

Peter has written his own faith story down.

Peter: When I was about twelve, I was staying with my grandparents who were Christians and who went to church regularly. My grandmother noticed that I did not want to go to church, so she said to me one day, "When God wants you He will call you". This really struck a chord with me and though I never told anyone, from that day forward I was waiting for God to call me. I moved to Australia when I was seventeen and whilst living in the bush at the age of nineteen, God called me. I always expected to hear a voice calling my name, but it came about in a different way. I started to notice that I was using the name Jesus in an inappropriate way, that's how it first started. I then met someone, who was a Christian, who lent me a book to read about the end times. After reading that, I bought a Bible and read the Gospel of John and for the first time ever, understood the Gospel that Christ had died to pay for all sin including mine. And I was desperate to be saved by Jesus. I felt then that a whole new world had opened up to me and was surprised how I had never seen or understood before as I was brought up in a Christian family with lots of input. It was like my mind had been blind to the Gospel. Then I joined a local church and got baptised in the middle of the bush, in the middle of nowhere, in Mount Newman, West Australia. Along with me there were quite a few other young people, about my age, who became Christians as well, it felt like a mini revival of God. I went to a prayer meeting one time round someone's house, I thought it would be the most boring thing in the world but it turned out to be an incredible experience.

Chapter 15: Fundraising doesn't always go to our plan but definitely to God's plan!

On my return, I tried to fundraise for the local workers new homes project and did some slide presentations and talks but was getting nowhere, plus I had some ill health keeping me from doing more. Then one day I went along to a small ladies meeting and talked about living conditions and the great work of Chengelo School which was giving a Christian education to the children of Zambia as a God given vision. One lady wrote a cheque out for Five Thousand Pounds, God bless her and I was over the moon to send it on to help the project have better living conditions. This is Christians working together making a difference, as Jesus said "I have come that they may have life and have it to the full."[15] One of my favourite Psalms tells us how much God loves his creation, "The Lord is gracious and compassionate... rich in love. The Lord is good to all" God's love is, simple, inclusive and beautiful.[16]

[15] Footnote: NIV Bible, John 10.10

[16] Footnote: NIV Gideons, Psalm 145.8-9.

Chapter 16: Dream Safari's & African Holiday our rewards!

Pete and I were blessed to go on safari regularly. On one occasion we were staying on the Serengeti plains and had been told that we must not venture out of the tent or camp at night. I can't remember what time it started but all night we were listening to lion's roaring and hyena's chuckling and they were encircling the camp it seemed to us, we were captivated, it was an incredible sound and a wonderful experience. The lion's sounded so powerful their roars coming from their stomachs, we listened and marvelled and our senses were heightened and we were reminded that these incredible creatures are at the top of the food chain out there on the plains of Africa!

In the dead of night I had a call of nature... Peter and I could not sleep anyway, so I gingerly opened up the zip of the two-manned tent by about four inches, as I did so I watched a hyena walking right past our tent, it was exhilarating, we were so excited! At that point, I quickly did the tent back up.

Later in the early morning it was fairly still outside now and I really needed to go to the toilet, so Pete and I made it to the outer edge of the camp, I was scared, it was still dark but I made it to tell the tale. The cleanest toilet in Africa is said to be behind a tree, everybody knows that. Thank the Lord for my angel that night who must have been very close and kept me safe. We found out in the morning that a Lion had boldly roamed into our camp and the guards had to scare it away with a warning gunshot!

I remember on this Safari lots of people passing us said they had seen elephant, up to this point on our trips we had not seen one and were desperate for a sighting. We didn't get the chance this time, but it's like that. Our guide drove up to a tree and a leopard was sitting majestically surveying us and the plains... we were so close we could even see his whiskers, it was thrilling. Then another time we were up early and stopped to wait for a Pride of female lions walking across the dirt track, who had red blood marks around their jaws. Another time we drove to some thicket and saw a cheetah and her cubs it was amazing seeing them play under the shade of the shrubbery. Whist on the Serengeti our vehicle nearly bumped into a Hippopotamus who was out of the water and if I had lent out of the car, I could have touched it, what a thrill that was.

What an honour to stand on the rim of the Ngorongoro Crater. We also went on Safari on the floor of the crater, it is so vast, I remember seeing the horn of a white rhinoceros in the distance.

We followed in Dr Livingston's footsteps a lot it seemed, the nineteenth century missionary doctor. We visited the Victoria Falls, that he named after Queen Victoria it was our local destination spot. We went to Lake Malawi and swam with the green, blue and gold fish there and marvelled at the sunsets. We travelled to Zanzibar, the "Spice Island" via a three day train journey through Tanzania passing vast nature reserves. We had our own cabin and it had a window to slide up by the table and one morning we were up early and going through a game reserve it was magical. There was a herd of giraffe, flying giant pelicans and at one point Pete pointed and said "look at that pile of stuff", I could hear his excitement but couldn't help saying "do you mean the herd of wilder beast?" It was like a scene from the beginning of time, the very beginning of creation it was such an honour. Thank you Lord, your creation is amazing. We arrived at the island of Zanzibar, we had taken a boat trip to get there from Dar es Salaam, we saw flying fish and dolphins swimming. We stayed on a beach, we had a tiny chalet with an outside shower but it was on one of the most beautiful deserted beaches that I ever saw with white fine sands and see-through crystal clear, warm waters, leading into pale, powdered blue waters. The sun was wonderfully hot and it all seemed like a dream come true.

We wrote a letter to Pete's Grandad who was ninety four at the time, he was a dear Christian man. My sister in law Sally read out our letter to grandad about all the work we were doing in Africa and the part about the hyena walking past the tent and the lions in the camp and he laughed and laughed and thought it was just great, Sally told us later. I think we made him proud, I hope so. We were not to see Grandad again this side of eternity God rest his soul but on our return, I remember we looked in the cemetery for grandad's grave, to pay our respects and the words came to mind "Why do you look for the living among the dead?" [17] I told Pete and we felt God's reassurance and comfort that day.

We journeyed on another break down to South Africa, to Johannesburg and stayed with Pete's cousin Lorraine and family for a few weeks. It was so weird and such a contrast to spend Christmas day in the sun and have Christmas dinner in the heat. We had a great time and

[17] Footnote: NIV Bible, Luke 24.5

the family became very special to us over our time there.

On one Safari we were sitting in a hide and one minute the watering hole was empty, it was vast, then very quickly it filled up with Elephants everywhere, I think about fifty to a hundred elephants and baby elephants and they moved without a sound. They were there then they were all gone, they had their drink or bath and disappeared. On another day, we went out with our friends, Alison and Ian, who were driving up an unmade road and suddenly came across a matriarch and her herd, she charged us and we reversed our vehicle so fast and made it out without harm, but the matriarch elephant was huge and mad at us, it certainly got our adrenaline going and we were thankful to be safe.

On one holiday we were nearing Mount Kilimanjaro, (don't mention it!) but it was cloudy and we did not get to see the iconic sight! Disappointing yes but not the end of the world or our trip!

In Africa, when we stepped out of the plane on a January day and the African sun was intensely shinning, it seems like everything you see is in amazing technicolour, they have blue birds instead of "little brown jobbies"[18] They have pink kingfishers instead of blue. They have vast red poinsettia bushes growing naturally instead of evergreens; Mauve jacaranda trees instead of plain green. I love nature and I love Essex, its rugged beauty and I'm glad to live there, I love nothing more than going for a long walk in the countryside but wow what a feast for your soul and spirituality to experience the continent of Africa. The baobab trees vast, pre historic kings of the rift valley are so different from any other tree that I ever saw, and my eyes couldn't stop gazing at them, one after another, they seemed other worldly and frankly insurmountable. On our journey in Malawi, we were driving up a steep incline and could see and hear eagles and then all of a sudden we were in the clouds looking over the African plains an uninterrupted view with no one else around, it felt a privilege to be there. These are amazing and unforgettable treasures. It's a wonderful world. In Africa we wore a coat that we brought from the UK twice! Even in winter by the afternoon we were in shorts and t-shirts.

[18] *Footnote: Bill Oddie quote '17 sept 2007 'what are little brown jobbies to the average person tend to be of the greatest interest' https://www.birdforum.net.*

Chapter 17: Sickness

Now I come to the part of the book where you will read about my broken dream. It all started about six months before I was due to leave Chengelo, I was aged thirty, I was experiencing heavy blood loss during my time of the month and I became anaemic and felt really tired most of the time. I went for blood tests and results appeared to be okay, however, I did not feel good, this eventually led me to have a D & C[19] operation in the Capital Lusaka. I went to a private hospital, I was absolutely petrified. The journey there was by a tiny single propelled plane, which was like an old style mini cooper. A kind farmer's son flew me down. It took an hour and half of flying to the capital. Boy were we high up in the vast African sky with nothing but dirt tracks, plains and jungle below. I felt very exposed up there not like travelling in a European jet.

Once at the hospital, something I shall never forget happened. After I had been prepared for surgery, I had to walk into the operating theatre having never had an operation before in my life. I vividly remember I was surrounded by stainless steel instruments. I was

[19] *Footnote: Dilation and curettage*

shocked at the quantity, they were hanging up all around the walls and I had to lie down, I shall say no more! Not like being in the prep room of a NHS room where you never see the theatre because you are asleep at this stage. My consultant had completed his training in the UK although one of my concerns was if I needed blood during the operation, what would be the source, my real concern was getting contaminated blood and contracting the HIV virus. I remember this was perhaps a neurotic fear, but there were many in our village that had Aids and it was looking back in the early nineties when medical knowledge was limited. I survived my ordeal thanks to my Consultant and did not need a transfusion, but unfortunately my health problems continued.

Subsequently, I left Chengelo five weeks early than the end of my contract and Peter and I discussed that he would stay on to mind the hostel until the end of term, which he did, it was a long five weeks. The parting at Lusaka was heart wrenching for us both, I really did not feel at all well and was worried that I would be poorly on the long, nine hour flight home. I felt quite insecure being so alone and having times of severe blood loss which was now continually happening. Praying and willing myself to sleep, thankfully I made it home without incident. My mum and brother Graham met me at the airport and I was so glad to be back in the UK.

Mum and I went to the hospital for them to check my blood and although my haemoglobin was low it was not a dangerous level. I made an appointment to see my doctor, he was not sympathetic to me, and he stood in front of me and stated that he was almost certain that I had a hormonal disorder that could only be treated with tablets. A conversation I think he was to regret, I pushed for a referral to the hospital and he finally relented to that.

Since my early years, aged eleven, I had always had sever period pain and heavy periods. I often felt like the lady in the Bible, with the issue of blood who had tried everything and reached out to touch Jesus and was amazingly immediately healed from Christ's power.[20] But my healing was to come through the NHS, in the early years my symptoms were controlled by hormonal treatment which had managed things.

After a consultation with my consultant at Basildon hospital, who I thank God for, he decided to proceed with a laparoscopy. The findings showed a Fibroid, the

[20] *Footnote: NIV Bible, Matthew 9.20-22*

size of a lemon! I was given a Zoladex injection into my stomach every month, this was harrowing! The injection came in a box, which I had to collect from the hospital dispensary. The box was approximately about thirty centimetres long and the doctor had to administer an anaesthetic into my stomach first so as to numb the area before giving me this large injection, needless to say I did not watch this procedure. The aim of this was to shrink the fibroid to a smaller size, it was clever but felt somewhat gruesome.

After three months I had a further operation to take a biopsy from the fibroid which came back clear. The bleeding still continued and sadly this led to a further operation to remove the fibroid. I thank God so much for the blessing of the NHS. At this time my haemoglobin was so low that I had to have a blood transfusion in order to be fit enough for this operation. My consultant removed the fibroid but it was a long and difficult operation to perform. Sadly, my symptoms were still not solved and my kind consultant said he needed to "turn the tap off" and I needed a hysterectomy. I was devastated as Peter and I had hoped for a family.

<u>My fifth and final operation</u>

I had asked for a private room, as I knew I was going to be all over the place emotionally after the surgery. I was checked in on a Sunday evening. The minutes and hours were long and I just kept praying. The fateful day arrived 20th April 1996. I woke early and went to look out of the window and there was a great big rainbow and no rain anywhere and I suddenly had a complete sense of total peace come over me. I knew it was a sign from God and I felt God was with me in that instant. My worries and nerves all vanished, so much so I did not need a pre-med, I felt fine, and I even remember that I was joking with the porters as they were taking me to the operation theatre. Since then I have seen others experience a God given peace in difficult situations too. God had not spared me the cruelty of this situation but He was with me and had spared my life. I will never know why God could not spare me this, but I trust that Jesus has been there at the lowest points, with me. My husband is and was a star, how he puts up with me is totally a gift of my life. Along with my parents and family, friends were the provision for me from God. I knew my Saviour Jesus had himself suffered greatly in his life on earth being flogged and subjected to a brutal death and he himself cried out to God, at point of death, "My God, my God, why have you forsaken me?"[21] There is some consolation knowing that you

[21] *Footnote: NIV Bible Matthew 27.46.*

follow and believe in a God who knows just how low life can take you on every level. Jesus was also betrayed in mind and soul, so God knows and with my faith I believe in a "in the twinkling of an eye"[22] Jesus and my heavenly father, will put all the wrongs to right one day. There are things we will never understand on this side of eternity, that is true but I faced the decision, did I give up on the hope of eternity and going forward without my God? I decided that I should in faith continue my journey through life, telling God all about the pain and sorrow.

The operation was completed and the pain afterwards was tremendous, I will never forget, I told myself "every minute that passes I am getting better", that is a good pep talk and it's true. At this time there was no key hole surgery or morphine button release gadgets to help me. Four days passed and I was released home and I recuperated at Peter's Parent's home.

It was just a routine check-up but my dear Sister in law Sally had asked if I would like her to come along with me, I said that it was my last check-up, but that she was

[22]*Footnote: NIV Bible 1 Corinthians 15.52*

welcome to come along, only God knew what was about to be said to me that day.

The God given Picture

As we were sitting in the waiting area, I said to Sally, I had a picture, in my mind's eye, very occasionally God guides and gives prior knowledge to an actual event and this was what was happening. The picture, vision, was telling me that one day Pete and I would be living in his Mum and Dad's cottage, on a four acre plot on a horticultural nursery in Battlesbridge, I remember, it seemed ludicrous at the time, but as Sally is a Christian I shared this with her. In hindsight, I believe that it was God's provision for us.

The routine check-up turned out to be devastating as the tests showed that I had low grade cancer cells. The consultant, I remember, struggled to tell me this news. Bless him for all that he had done for me, Sally dissolved into tears, bless her for her love. I managed to hold it together and to drive home, once there in the arms of Pete the tears came like a flood. It felt like we were in total free fall, the bottom had fallen out of our world.

It was like someone had hit me hard in the face and I was then completely numb. I needed some space and time to process all this, I needed God. What on earth was happening to me, to us? I just could not take it all in. Peter and I over the months had visited various places for prayer, we had prayed and fasted, but the situation was going from bad to worse, it was a living nightmare, it felt like hell on earth. I was told I needed three weeks of radiotherapy at Southend Hospital.

In my experience, God does not always take away our sicknesses or sorrows but he does provide for us, in them. One of my favourite films is about the a missionary called Gladys Aylward who felt called to China and who saved one hundred orphaned children, during the Japanese invasion, by taking them over mountains to safety. I do not know if Gladys Aylward actually said these words or if it was poetic license in the film but they are profound. Ingrid Bergman is playing Gladys and is offering help to the Mandarin played by Robert Donat and Chief Prison Guard, after the Chief Guard says "I hear your God protects you from harm... you go in" and Gladys, in the film says "It is safety of the soul my faith promises, not the body... I will go in" and she successfully stops the riots. Wow what a beautiful truth and pearl of wisdom.[23] This firm moves me to tears every time.

Another truth I have found God makes up for when nature and life go wrong, in the Bible passage Joel 2 it says "I will repay you for the years the locusts have eaten."[24] God has definitely made it up to me and I can say God has been so faithful and if he can do it for me, He can do it for you whatever the circumstances or difficult times you have fallen on, God is one prayer away. One fact is that I have learnt, if we trust Him, God brings good out of the bad times in our lives this is wonderful news and can lead to a fulfilling, abundant life.

[23] Footnote: Film about Gladys Aylward a maid who felt called by God to go to China, 'The Inn of the Sixth Happiness', (1957, Twentieth Century Fox, A CinemaScope Picture)

[24] Footnote: NIV Bible Joel 2.25.

Chapter 18: Neighbours who needs them!

After my operation we returned to our Laindon Link
flat, we had been having dreadful neighbour problems
from the guy above us, who had his music playing till
the early hours of the morning and when we
approached him about it the situation got worse. It got
so bad that we had to move our mattress in to our
living room and we wore earplugs but could still hear
the music. Once he went out leaving the music blearing
out and playing all night. It was unbearable, we not
only had the tragedy of my operation and recovery to
deal with but all this too it was like torture.

I can't remember when but Peter's parents moved and
asked us if we would live at the cottage and look after
the place for two years for them. We jumped at the
opportunity and it meant Pete would be close at hand
working at the nursery. We moved during my
radiotherapy, and Pete and friends Shirley and Les
thankfully helped move all of our belongings out of our
flat.

God's vision, picture and knowledge given to me on the
day of diagnosis came to pass, we moved to the Nursery
at Battlesbridge. God had made a way through the
awfulness. Thank you Lord.

Later in life, we have spent now over twenty years living by the River Crouch, and our neighbours Pauline and her late husband Ray who really are worth their weight in gold to us. And all our lovely neighbours around us are such a blessing to us as a family.

Chapter 19: My Heart and Body were Broken

I got angry and I now understand that anger is a part of the grief process, but when it came it surprised me. I had a visit from a Macmillan nurse, at first I was so angry, I did not want to see her, after all I thought what good could she possibly do me, as my whole world had already totally fallen apart. Since the operations and cancer news, the passing hours and days were perhaps some of the lowest moments of my life. The Nurse sat downstairs and I remember thinking, "who could I turn to? Who could give me the relief that I needed from this living hell?" I decided to meet her, but I was not going to need her I remember thinking to myself, I think now what was happening to me, in rejecting this cancer specialist nurse, I was in some way rejecting the realisation of the cancer that I had had. Strange how your feelings and mind react to trauma and heart ache. Small mercies, I was told by the hospital that the surgery had removed all the cancer and the radiotherapy treatment was precautionary, the Consultant called it a "belt and braces" procedure.

This was such a lonely time for me as Peter, had to go to work of course and go about growing plants and he could not stay at home indefinitely. Fortunately, I was right near him at the cottage as the nursery was next door. He would pop indoors to see how I was doing during his breaks. I remember at one time I was feeling incredibly low, that no one could help me, not even Pete. My body was broken and my heart too and I could see no future and had no hope. I had wanted my own children and this was now never to be and I had to come to terms with that fact. It was around this time that I experienced suicidal thoughts but Pete held on to me somehow, thank you husband.

Through this painful time I developed a coping Strategy for my depression and I only share it in the hope it may help another suffering soul. My circumstantial depression was like a big black cloud coming towards me and would make me feel a sense of foreboding. When the depression was over me, and with me it was a feeling like being terrified and had a sense of total helplessness, and loss of hope about it. Once I was in the thick of it, in its grasp, it would take me down, like a spiral and down and down like, to the bottom of a dark pit. It was a frightening place to be, total desolation, and it felt like a hell or how I imagine "Hell" to be, with its total absence of peace and keen feelings of total absence from my God.[25] At some points during this time, I could not be alone, I remember sitting drawing cats around my Mum and Dad's home! I learnt to sense the depression coming over me and I found a diversion strategy, I would tell Pete and we would go out for example for tea, usually Mc D's. I found that at such times to just be in different surroundings, either in family or a friend's homes, would make the 'going down the spiral effect' limited and the depression would leave me, till the next episode. And so I kept on trying not to hit rock bottom and with some success. I am a lucky soul in many ways, as that is the only depression that I have ever suffered, and I am very thankful for that. I think depression is far worse than my cancer and illnesses that I have suffered in my life.

I felt that my body had been mutilated and the sacred part of me violated, all my prospects were grim, this was my view at the time, as I had wanted a baby. What made it worse was also that everyone knew my

[25] *Footnote: Feelings and the facts can be contradictory, as in my healthy state of mind, I know God is always there, in NIV Bible, Hebrews, 13.5 which I had often held on to passionately believing, 'God has said, Never will I leave you, never will I forsake you'.*

business and what had happened to me, I wanted to run and hide from the awful truth of my life. I was isolated by my experience being only thirty one years old and I felt incredibly insecure, I had been shaken to the very core and I was bereaved for the children I would never have.

At the time, I had six Sister-in-laws, I have three brothers and Pete has three sisters, God bless them all but somehow every time they became pregnant it highlighted my own loss and it was like I would have to go back to square one again emotionally. In no way did I ever let it be known and these dear Sisters-in-laws had their own destinies to follow, I knew that and wished them well and the new nieces and nephews were very sweet.

I felt that God had left me, I remember feeling angry at God for not taking proper care of me, but with every day that passed I would look out of my window and see the beautiful country fields, sunshine, flowers and birds singing and I just could not deny that God had created it all, although my faith was hanging on by a thread. I remember I could not pray at this time.

At this time I had a visit from my faithful friend Doreen, who once before had helped us going to Africa. She visited me and listened to what I had to say, she said one thing that I shall never forget, "Jane all you have to do is survive!" she meant all I had to do was survive each minute and each hour, not live but survive, I felt I could manage this prospect and to survive. What she was saying made sense I could only exist and survive right now because I was deeply wounded. Believe me, it took all of my might to survive and I did it, but the pain, emotionally, psychology were worse than the cancer and post-operative pain, the tears and the broken heart that I had was the most painful thing of all in my suffering. My friend said another thing which I will pass on for it may help someone else suffering, she said to me that "we were not created to have a broken heart ever or a broken body ever, the human condition was made and created originally to live forever. God made it a perfect world and there was no death, in his plan." So when the heart aches, the body is scarred and the mind is depressed with grieving we are broken as humans. Literally we break down because the pressure is just too much. I could manage just surviving somehow, it felt like a relief. Thank you Doreen for your amazing wisdom, I have used this in my ministry to take burdens off of people's shoulders too, like you did for me that day.

Those black days of mine lasted for six months and very slowly and gradually my life healed and improved. The bleak days were no longer an everyday experience as I woke, but every other day and then just every now and then. I grew stronger both in heart, spirit, mind and body again. I then started living again.

Chapter 20: Radiotherapy

The preparation day for the radiotherapy was harrowing for me after all my operations and examinations and I really struggled that day to undertake the necessary examinations and procedures needed. Imagine I was still healing from major surgery it was just six weeks after my surgery. I was tattooed with tiny dots, to indicate for the radiographer the correct placement and again examined it was a total nightmare, it hurt in every way imaginable, physically and psychologically. I do not know to this day how I managed it. Soon afterwards I started my three week course of radiotherapy, and fifteen days set for treatment.

I walked in to a pink waiting room, piped music was playing, I remember thinking "oh no", this is bright and cheerful, I wanted gloom to match the foreboding that I felt. I did not wish to accept my condition and I certainly did not wish to be present in these surroundings. I struggled being in the waiting room every time waiting for my turn, I hated it, and I saw that I was the only young person there. I guess, what I really was feeling was the injustice of being just thirty one years old and battling cancer, as I said I was angry, in denial and resistant, which Elizabeth Kubler-Ross developed a model which includes her five stages of grief.[26] These have helped so many people, to understand their bereavement over the years, so as not to be isolated in the thick of it, but know that most people in bereavement have similar feelings in their grief and that it is normal to get angry and depressed.

I hope they can help someone reading this book too, I wholly recommend the model. That is why I have written this book, firstly God told me to and told me to get on with it, my hope is that in the pages of this book, my story just might help someone out there in their journey.

Going back to the pink room, I remember refusing to sit in the seated area provided and I stood by the window with my back towards the reception area waiting to be called. That's how bad it was to be there, I couldn't face it.

I was trying to block out the situation and I just had to do it. I remember it took all the strength I had to stay there, I felt overcome and just really wanted to escape but somehow I found out what brave means. To face something you fear and deal with it anyway. "Well done", to my thirty one year old self from your

[26] *Footnote: Appendix 2*

fifty five year old self!

The side effects of the first week of radiotherapy were hardly detectable, however by the end of the second week I was beginning not to be able to muster up any energy and by the third week I was unable to stand or wash my own hair. I was feeling totally exhausted. I started to get a burning sensation inside my stomach; it was like an intense spasm pain which would double me over. The Consultant told me it was irritable bowel syndrome caused by the actual burning of the therapy. He said, it should vanish after the treatment has stopped, but I still had two more treatments to go and the pain became unbearable. I simply could not endure anymore and we agreed to call it a day. I hasten to add everyone is different when it comes to radiotherapy and not everyone has such extreme difficulties.

As I settled home, it was then that I stopped eating as it agitated my stomach too much and made the pain so severe, I remember that it also became difficult to drink anything too. The radiotherapy was continuing its work inside my stomach, it was literally burning away anything that could be sinister but then I went downhill dramatically. I remember being awake in the night with the pain, reeling in fact, then the sickness began and it would not stop, a convulsion would take hold of my whole body and kept on happening. I was still not able to drink I had already lost a lot of weight due to the lack of nourishment but now the process of dehydration begun and by the early hours of the morning Peter called the doctor who called an ambulance. I hate to be so graphic but due to my insides being burnt I could not pass water easily either and now this was causing great distress, I had a temperature and still being sick, bringing up bile only.

The ambulance arrived, once I had been stabilised Basildon hospital arranged for me to be taken to Southend hospital to have x-rays and I was told that I had somehow picked up a viral infection. And for a usually healthy soul this is bearable, but of course I had no immune system left, the only medication they could give me was an intravenous saline drip and intravenous anti-sickness drug which did work and I was very grateful for.

My Macmillan Nurse later said that I was in a desperate state and that it could have been fatal. Believe me I felt near to death. I remember laying there awake the whole time just feeling so incredibly weak, thinking that I wanted to give in and give up.

It was like one blow after another, just how much could a human being take! I do not know how I pulled back from that point to recovery but I did. I did have two very special people that did not want me to give up, my dear friend Shirley and my husband Pete. They visited me alternately and helped me through and I know God was there too. I got better very slowly, all I was focusing on was on physically getting well.

I went to a friend's home when I came out of hospital, the Remmington's home to convalesce, as my parents did not have the room and Peter was busy moving us from the flat to the cottage. With tender care, I slowly got better. I was still unable to eat at first, due to the therapy and painful bowel and so I was prescribed food drinks from the hospital, after a while I remember starting off with a small piece of Yorkshire pudding, at this stage I must have been about six and a half stone. I am indebted to these dear friends forever for all their loving care.

Chapter 21: Chaplaincy

It took sometime before I went back to full time work, possibly two years. I started off with an ironing job at home. Then worked in a clothes shop Mackey's part-time which I enjoyed and then finally went to work as a secretary temping in the City. One evening as I was travelling home, I was having a quiet time praying and reading my Bible notes, I sensed a calling to Chaplaincy work and that I should get in contact with an old friend from college days, Revd Ann Stevenson, who was a Hospital Chaplain at City Hospital, Birmingham. Now I have to say here that when God speaks to you it is just amazing, it is like you're walking on air, there is a sense that you are about to embark upon the best thing that you have ever done.

My friend Ann was the Chaplain for twenty six years and is now retired after many years of service. Back then I contacted her, we planned for my visit for a week. I remember explaining to Ann that whilst I felt interested in the work, "I did not want to visit the baby ward, oncology ward or the mortuary" and remember to this day her words "Well Jane, if you are interested in Chaplaincy work you will have to visit all those wards," and so I did, I had an excellent week and as I ventured to go on to the wards I had some wonderful times listening and meeting people. So during this week it became evident that this work was for me and just visiting there for one week was a wonderful therapeutic experience for me.

During the week I also visited my old Bible College. The Staff there were very welcoming and glad to see me, as the college staff and pupils had been praying for me during my illness. We had a wonderful time catching up and then the Principal prayed for me. After the prayer I felt renewed inside and remember phoning Pete from a pay phone across the street and mentioned that I had been feeling dead inside for so long, but that after the prayer I felt spiritually that there was a light inside of me, like a flame that had been rekindled, I actually felt renewed and healed in my emotions.

Some months later Peter mentioned that, he had noticed that I no longer got upset when seeing babies or pregnant mums and that God must truly have healed me. The feelings of grief and pain had all completely gone and have never returned since. I believed that God healed me emotionally that week. Praise Him.

On my return I contacted the local hospital Broomfield, as I had decided that I would not go to a hospital where I had been a patient. I attended an interview for a Lay

Chaplain's role and shortly after some training and shadow work I was given two wards to visit on a weekly basis, visiting approximately fifty patients a week. This work became very dear to me and in the weeks to follow I was commissioned Lay Ward Chaplain by the Arch Deacon from the Cathedral. I undertook this work for five years.

During this time it was a great privilege to visit the sick and dying, to minister to them through prayer and administering Holy Communion or simply by sitting and listening. The team that I worked with were a special group of people and I became very fond of them all. We enjoyed quiet retreat days, along with training days together. I think as a person I have grown in a lot of ways and the work is very close to my heart. To this day I have seen how God has taken my experience of being broken physically, spiritually and mentally and used it for good in helping others. I discovered that often I found I could cut across many barriers with the odd sentence indicating that I had suffered too and whilst I was not them in their circumstances it would seem to give comfort and hope knowing that I was acquainted with the process of suffering and loss. So I can say Praise God for giving me this work and to be a witness to His healing and presence in so many of the rooms and wards at the hospital.

Chapter 22: Waltham Abbey

Peter and I had been asked to sing at a friend's Induction, Diana, as curate at Waltham Abbey, along with Angela also a volunteer chaplain. Diana also worked as part of the Broomfield Chaplaincy team and she had heard us singing the then new version of *"The Lord's my Shepherd"* by Stuart Townsend[27] and asked us to sing on her special day. We were of course delighted to oblige at the Abbey!

The day arrived and Waltham Abbey looked beautiful. Angela, Pete and I got there early so as to warm up our voices and tune the guitar and organise the amplifier for the big event. The Abbey started to fill up and we were ready in our little spot. Just as the service started twenty five members from the Abbey's choir entered in a mass of red flowing robes and then the three of us looked at each other feeling rather insignificant, their singing was amazing let us not understate this. Our time came and we sung from our hearts, Diana was pleased afterwards which was all that mattered to us. All I can say is chalk and cheese from one genre to the total opposite... but how we praised God and how we

[27] *Footnote: You can listen on you tube*

laughed and amused ourselves on the way home. You
never know what God can do with you and where you
might go, if you are only willing!

Chapter 23: The Degree

It stretched my brain muscles and brought great joy and also tears along the way. I had writers block on at least two occasions which incapacitated me for months on end. I enjoyed the reading, module work and the practical along with the reading of history. It was the essay's that I struggled with. My sincere thanks to friends Reg Luhman and Dawn for all your kind support.

Finally, after many part-years of study, on the 3rd December 2008, at Cheltenham Race course no less, I was dressed for my graduation, the photos taken I sat in the royal enclosure surveying the racecourse, it was a beautiful sunny day and a stunning spectacle actually. As I waited for my turn to shake Lord Carey's hand, former Arch Bishop of Canterbury George Carey, I felt amazement that I had made it and my dearest Pete managed to get a photo of me, shaking the Universities Chancellor's hand. It was an incredible memory.

Chapter 24: Back to the Beginning and Full Circle

Around 1997, I had started my long distance learning with the Open Theological College and at a later date this college was to merge and come under the University of Gloucestershire and in another twist of destiny my life had come full circle when I collected my degree. That was the only time that I visited my birth county. There was such a contrast of the grandeur of my graduation day to some streets and humble rows of workers cottages that I visited that day and felt my entrance into the world had been in very simple settings surrounded by beautiful countryside.

After visiting Gloucestershire I wanted to visit Coram a children's home when I had been a baby in London. Known as the foundlings hospital founded by Sir Thomas Coram, 1739, a Naval Captain, who was moved by seeing babies dying on the streets of London and felt God move him to provide a home for them. The story goes he approached the great and the good of London and even George Frideric Handel, composer was a Patron and used to play every year at a fundraiser. As a premature baby my entrance in to the world was pretty dramatic with my grandfather helping my mother with my birth, a miracle really. When I visited Coram they were able to give me this information along with some baby photos of myself and letters hand written by my birth mum that were given to me, I was really glad for the visit, thank you to everyone past and present at Coram for everything. Although sitting there in this place where I was connected at such a distant beginning somehow felt bizarre that this was my first ever home in the world and looking out of the window and at the children's soft play area below I had a sense of how vulnerable life can truly be and how vulnerable I had been there.[28] I do hope that both my biological parents went on to have happy and fulfilled lives. I believe one day I will meet them in Jesus' kingdom. But, forty four years later, who would have said, that I would be graduating at the University of Gloucestershire the very county that I was born in. I hope that my maternal Grandad would have been proud of me.

[28] *Footnote.www.coram.org.uk*

Chapter 25: The Adoption

In 1999 Pete and I had our first interview for the adoption process with Barnardo's and after completing all of the training we were successful eventually in our application to panel for adoption of two children. However, the search was like an emotional roller coaster and it took its toll on Pete and I, till one day we decided to discontinue.

We then decided to get a dog to join our two cats Nartasha and Sarna, whose names are from the Zambian Bemba dialect 'Nartasha Sarna' meaning: 'Thank you very much'. Pete bought me a wonderful Christmas present my Dalmatian puppy Rosie, who I completely adored and she shared our lives and gave us so much love, Rosie was our eternal toddler and we all lived together for thirteen and a half wonderful years. Tasha and Sarna our gentle black cats lived till age seventeen and nineteen. Here's a good theological question "Do animals go to heaven?" I say "yes" and I look very much forward to seeing all my girls again and being with them forever. There is a fabulous poem called Rainbow Bridge, all about the heavenly reunion with our fur babies and I have often shared it in ministry.[29] A year past and we decided that we would look in to fostering as we could not see our lives without children. But during this time we came to the conclusion that it was not fostering that we wanted, but to indeed adopt children of our own. Our Social Worker was very experienced and we continued with her support. She had been on the telephone to a colleague who mentioned, as she was about to finish their call, "do you know anyone who is looking for two little girls?" which she replied that she did actually.

Soon there were two little children needing a "forever Mummy and Daddy", as the professionals put it. We proceeded with the interviews and before too long we were meeting the foster parents and then after several meetings it was planned for the children to come and move in with us. This time it was meant to be, our destiny. This was our rainbow. We are now the parents of two lovely adult daughters Amber and Chloe.

Amber and Chloe you brought much joy and laughter into our lives and I know that we won't just be together for this life but I know in my heart, we will be together

[29] *Footnote: See Appendix 3 Rainbow Bridge Poem*

forever one day in God's kingdom. I hope you liked going to school by the river and enjoyed village life, we always tried to give you all the opportunities, to make life as nice as possible. With a lot of love and forgiveness, as a family, with hard work on both sides, we made it. As any parent tells you, children can take you to your limits and we have had our moments, as I am sure many adopted families have experienced, but more often than not there are real blessings and it feels absolutely fulfilling to be Mum and Dad. I would never have changed it, Pete and I love the girls to bits. I thank God for all the people involved with the adoption who helped to make our dream come true, thank you to the staff at Barnardo's, Colchester branch. And a special heartfelt thank you to our dear families and closest friends who have helped us along the way, for your never failing love and support. There is a saying, it takes a community to raise children and that is certainly true for us.

I guess we were good enough parents, my friend said that to me once and it was very helpful, you just have to be "a good enough Mum" and not getting it right all of the time, these are relieving words for any parent. God often intervened over the years, telling me what to do and giving me wisdom and unconditional love and forgiveness for the girls and thankfully they gave it back too.

Amber I am so proud of you on the day of your baptism, 8th September 2013 at Central Baptist, Chelmsford. When you gave your story of faith to over three hundred people and Dr Revd Paul Beasley Murray, our wonderful Pastor and I, baptised you in the Name of Father, Son and Holy Spirit, in the baptism pool. It was such a blessing and a highlight that day we shared it as a whole family and enjoyed cake with church family afterwards.

Chloe so proud of you when you gave birth, to our first granddaughter, Lily-Mae with just gas and air and I will never forget cutting Lily's cord just after she was born, thank you. And I shall never forget the drive through McD's you asked me take you through just hours before giving birth, it makes me smile now.

Dear Lilian, Shirley's mum, who was like another mum to me and used to tell me "the only thing that really matters in life, is that we help each other through", which is so true and beautifully simple, it has been a guideline for my adult life and I have often used it myself too. I often reflect, how often it is the little things that people do or say that help turn us and our situations around and make that real difference.

Chapter 26: Pastor Jane Guest

The journey to being called as Pastor of Leigh Beck Baptist was a blessing to me. I had felt a call to preach the Gospel of Christ even when I had been at Bible College aged twenty four, but back then women were not allowed to. This call to preach never really went away and I went preaching whenever the opportunity arose. In Revelation it says that "God opens doors that no one can shut and closes doors no can open" so true.[30] It took lots of faith and patience on the road to becoming a Minister of the Gospel of Christ.

I made enquiries about where I could preach and soon, I had eight churches with regular preaching during the year, I was out preaching about twice a month. Leigh Beck Baptist, Canvey Island was among them. One Harvest festival service I felt God's Holy Spirit move powerfully amongst us during my preaching and God moved some of us to tears, (and yes my preaching can have that affect but I'm afraid I can't take the credit for this time) and following that service many people started asking whether I could be the new Pastor at Leigh Beck. After prayer and going through the church

[30] *Footnote: NIV Bible Revelation 3.7.*

members meeting it was voted on and the following March 7th, 2006, I started serving there as Pastor and I loved it. The people of Canvey Island are a great community of people, they speak as they find and are generous in spirit and hospitality and have big hearts and they will always have a place in my heart.

That September we hosted the Alpha course. I began door to door work, with my sister in law Sally and saw the life transforming work of the Lord. People were starting to have faith in Jesus Christ and their lives were being transformed as a result, it was beautiful to see. We would often be baptising four people at a time. They were also being welcomed in to membership and in three years we had twenty three new Christians. I can only explain it this way, that as we set the scene and had done the preparation work, I remember all the ladies in the church would cook a hot meal and a desert on a rota, families would set the tables beautifully, thank you ladies for getting behind this work, God bless you. God would use the Alpha course and we watched as people experienced God's love and acceptance. I was preaching both morning and evening and leading the whole service too, I poured out my heart and soul. Grandparents started bringing grandchildren regularly, new converts were bringing their entire families and babies and children were being dedicated, we had weddings.

It got to the stage that the ninety chairs we had in the church were not enough and at one church meeting one member said that they would be happy to purchase one new chair and this begun a chain reaction and before we knew it we had twenty brand new chairs on order, it was exciting times. And I will always be grateful that I served the lovely people of Canvey and want to say thank you for your care and love to me and my family. I even took my first of everything there wedding and baptism, dedication and funeral. Besides all this we undertook as a team, Holiday Clubs, schools work and youth work. We had a thriving mum and toddler group "Tot stop" for young families too. The life blood was flowing throughout the week now, Monday to Friday we were open for prayer time and that's I believe the foundation for it all, to God be the Glory great things He has done.

Chapter 27: The Valley of Death

Psalm 23 "Thou I walk through the valley of Death"!

I remember that I had visited the Tuesday fellowship group and joined them for their summer tea party and enjoyed strawberries and cream, we all had a great time. The church knew how to put on a great spread always. That evening, I began to feel very unwell with a fever, and asked Pete to go out and get me some cocodamol, which he did and I felt so bad that I cried the kids were in bed and it took Pete a considerable time to buy the tablets. On his return we phoned 111 and a doctor called and said that I could do with going to A & E but the kids were in bed, you know how it is. So the whole night I had struggled through and just slept on the sofa, which was odd. I visited my doctor the following morning who told me that I had developed a touch of pneumonia and that I could go home with antibiotics or go up to hospital the choice was mine. Peter and I looked at one another and we decided to go to hospital, this turned out to be a very significant decision.

After examinations at the local general hospital I was taken to critical care, and felt like I was very disorientated, the fact was I was in a rapid decline of health. I was not responding to the antibiotics and felt very ill. I remember saying my goodbye to Pete and that "I had peace and that I had done everything in life that I had wanted to and that I wanted a happy funeral." Shortly after this, I was put onto a ventilator, a life support machine. My vital organs were now closing down and the machine was breathing for me. At one point my lungs had collapsed and my kidneys stopped functioning, my heart and brain were the two remaining organs working. I had Pneumococcal Streptococcus bacterium Pneumonia and the Consultant prepared Pete for the worst and gave me and Pete a moment.

This is what happened next, it is a little difficult to describe, I was sort of in a vision within myself, in my spirit. I ventured to a grey place and I felt unhappy to be there, I remember looking around and saying to God that "if this is it? I give you my heart and soul", it seemed almost instantaneously to change and I felt what was like ribbons of love and light going through my whole body and a sensation of going upwards, I felt showered with love, never felt such love on earth, it was perfect and it was heavenly. Then before me, the sun was shining and the sky was bright blue and I recognised the place where I was, Hullbridge Park by the river, but I was up high and not alone God was by my side. The grass looked a bright spring green and as I looked from above I saw my husband and the girls and our dog Rosie all having a picnic down on the field right next to the river Crouch and I heard God say to me "Is this what you want?" and at that point I knew it was, I wanted my little family. I am not sure how long or at what point this all happened, but that vision from then on never went away. I felt God had given me a choice to stay with him or go back to my family. Believe me the feelings of great love, were like ribbons of light and love flowing through my whole body it was pretty amazing and nice to be there. Being there seemed much more real than life here somehow. I kept telling myself that the vision could be mine if I really wanted it and somehow I had to fight for it. I also kept saying Psalm 23 to myself over and over and the Lord 's Prayer afterwards.

I can hardly tell you how hard the next hours and days were. I was insecure at night and awake as I had slept in the day and so I was watching the moon move slowly around the summer night sky, going in and out of consciousness. I remember one nurse would come and sit with me and tell me everything was going to be all right she gave me comfort. Another night my night nurse gave me his music to listen to on his iPod and take my mind off things. The intuition of a specialist nurse is incredible, there I was couldn't speak and yet they knew

I was struggling and I was feeling totally insecure and helpless and was shown such tender care. A tracheotomy was inserted into my wind pipe I could only communicate by writing, but the drugs made it almost impossible to get my hand moving. During the day I would work at breathing for my life, I would have to endure breathing through tubes that blew against my breath that would strengthen my lungs, it was almost impossible; it lasted for an hour and half at a time. It was a bit like putting your head outside of the car window when moving, as a child and you couldn't breathe. It felt like torture but necessary for life to start over. On one occasion, I had a blockage of mucus and could not get any air and could not speak and had to do all I could to get the nurses attention for help, it was horrible and very frightening. I had learnt to unblock the tube but this wouldn't budge.

I knew that I needed to get moving and that I needed to sit upright. The day came when three physiotherapists and two nurses moved me with ventilator tubes into a harness whilst still on the bed, I had been lying down now for two and half weeks, it took all my energy to help myself with the aid of a harness. I sat in the chair for a full half an hour, feeling utterly exhausted and watching the clock hands move slowly round for the duration just longing to be back in bed. The next few days I sat for one hour and so it went. The day came when I could be tested to see if I could come off of the ventilator. I had to successfully sip a drink of water down, bearing in mind I was still being fed through a nose tube. I remember feeling worried about this and was most concerned wishing more than anything to come off the trachea device attached to my windpipe. There was a lot riding on this test as each attachment disappeared it equalled my getting better and nearing to the door and to my freedom and desired destination home. I am indebted to the Critical Care Team, they worked hard to save my life, thank you forever. When I was in critical care I expressed a need to move my legs as they ached. I was used to walking my Dalmatian dog miles and I felt like I needed to get them moving again. The physiotherapists brought me a pair of pedals on a frame that I could place my feet and cycle on the spot. I set myself twenty pedals, three times a day and increased this to thirty pedals then forty by the end. I was still not walking but I could pedal one hundred and fifty spins a day. I just knew the more I could move the quicker it would be to get home to my family who I was missing dreadfully.

The day came when I was taken down to the respiratory ward, the only tube I had was the feed tube. I was still weak and had to be helped to walk. By this time I had not walked for over three weeks. If I were to explain it felt like everything was being done for the very first time, breathing unaided, sitting up, walking, exercising it was strange, my body was just that weak. It was all so difficult. Pete was brilliant always there, supporting me through, I would watch the clock on the wall till his visits, he would read short stories from magazines to me, just sit and hold my hand whilst I listened to music through headphones and slept and he would tape the latest Wimbledon match on a video cassette and I remember the junior doctors having a look in too. So from the brink of death and what the Bible calls the valley of the shadow of death I was given a choice by God and I took it. I crawled back gradually to life. I was meant to be on the ward for a couple of weeks, which ended up being just four days and sent home with oxygen which wasn't necessary in the end. I had experienced some critical care psychosis whilst on the ward, these were terrifying day time dreams, they were living nightmares, I'd rather not mention them but I can remember them to this day, they made me feel a foreboding feeling of being frightened, it was the side effects of all the medications. My dear family stood by me and many clergy friends prayed for me, my thanks to special friends Revd Paul Stow and Revd David Keeble who left the Eastern Baptist Association Conference to come and pray with me in person on the ward, I was out of it and don't remember much, I remember how Revd Gordon Bates used to visit me regularly and say a comforting short prayer for me. Nationwide friends and church family prayed for my recovery and our prayers were answered Praise God. Thank you Lord, for the NHS and giving me the choice to come back.

After my illness, John Kennett, Singer Songwriter, Pastor and formally my worship leader, from Leigh Beck Baptist days wrote this song for me, thanks John, bless you, what an honour.

"Faith Can Move Mountains."
Faith can move mountains, Faith can move mountains;
You can't find a way through;
God will do it for you... Faith can move mountains.

When the way, before us seems too hard to bear;
The answer to all our needs is prayer;
For there is nothing God cannot do;
Because of his love for you... Faith can move
mountains...

We believe in God's word there'll come a day;
When all things on earth will pass away;
Our mountains we'll cast into the sea; Then we'll praise
Him for all eternity... Faith can move mountains... [31]

[31] *Footnote: CD 'Held in the Fathers Hands' by John Kennett &
friends. John is now a Reverend and Chaplain at Havens Hospices*

Chapter 28: A move towards Palliative Care

Pete is always telling me, you go through life changing ill health patches but don't change your life. No I tend to get up, if God allows, brush myself down and carry on again. But I guess to come through a life changing experience like that and not expect change in your life is a little naive. My Church had prayed and had worked hard in my absence. The road to recovery was not an easy one and when winter came I had one chest infection after another. I was working hard and doing my very best trying to complete my final essay for my Bachelor of Arts honours degree in Theology; not easy when your brain is like mush. Coming through that winter it became apparent in the March, that I could no longer continue as Minister at the church and so sadly I had to say farewell to the church family there. After working my three month notice I left in the July. I will always look back on my season at Leigh Beck as a great privilege and opportunity to become a Baptist Minister and to serve the people of Canvey. God showed me and confirmed to me at this church, that your gender does not matter to him, as a minister it is your willing spirit that he cares about and to help His kingdom come. I often see my friends, dear Rachel, a real soul mate, I thank God for you and your friendship. And I have been back to the Church to take a funeral and to attend the ordinations of my friends John and Dave. As I handed in my resignation on the 27th April it was with a heavy heart but knowing it was the only way forward for me. I gave my life over to God for what was to happen next and then days later I applied for the post of Havens Hospices Chaplain on the 30th April. Two interviews later, I was successful in obtaining a new job as full time Chaplain. I left the church and had two weeks annual leave and started at the Hospices on the 7th September 2009. I sensed God honoured my hard work at Leigh Beck and in his love and grace to me. What a faithful God we serve.

Chapter 29: The Ordinand

What a day, 6th March 2010, my ordination service was
to be such a blessing, with all my family and friends in
attendance there to wish me well, the service was at
Avenue Baptist Church, Southend on Sea. John, Steve
and Janet from Leigh Beck worship group all played for
my ordination service, along with Revd Phil and it was a
joy. Avenue Baptist is a beautiful church, thank you for
granting my request to hold my ceremony there. My
new title from that day forward Reverend Jane Guest
and I am so filled with gratitude. The church was full
and as I stood at the platform door, out of sight waiting,
the organist Janet played "Jesus Joy of man's desire", I
felt overwhelmed and remembered this tune from my
wedding day and now my ordination day, completely
both times not organised by me, but by a wonderful
creative faithful, loving heavenly Father. I was so
happy, this day was a dream come true.

Chapter 30: Baptist Union Accreditation

As a family we went up to the Blackpool Baptist Union Assembly in 2013 and it was there that I got my official handshake and full accreditation as a Minister of the Baptist Union of Great Britain, it was truly amazing. All the years of study and interviews, ministerial recognition committees, and selection conferences later, here I was, it was thrilling. My special thanks to the Eastern Baptist Association, Revd Paul Hills and Revd Sheila Martin for all your support over many years. After my degree I had gone on to complete my three more years of learning contract with Spurgeon's in October 2012, as a Newly Accredited Minister. At the accreditation service the renowned speaker Revd Malcolm Duncan spoke from the book of Philippians about the importance of '"Shining like stars" for the Gospel of Christ' what a lovely aspiration, I was on cloud nine, and this was another dream come true. Praise be to God.

Chapter 31: The Dilemma – "Was my Book for my relations only?"

Why did I put my book down and do nothing with it, well, I suppose looking back, it just wasn't the right time yet, I pushed the door and it closed. The question being was my book for my relations only? But whilst I was sitting at my computer in the Chaplaincy office, before leaving Havens, I felt God bring to my mind again, my book, the one He had told me to write. To be real honest with you, I could never think my story was that remarkable to be writing a book about my life, but faithfully I believe maybe God wants someone to hear my story. I sensed God was reminding me and that He was wanting me to do something more with it. Then I was chatting to a Fair Havens Nurse as we were making a cuppa and we got talking and I mentioned about maybe doing something with a book that I had written nine years ago. She told me about her mum who had written a book. It turned out that I knew her Mum, Angela, and had worked with her on a Schools Assembly Team in Basildon some twenty five years earlier. Back then Angela wanted to write a book and do a degree, she actually wrote her book and got three degrees. Angela kindly sent her book for me to read "How to be a Super Ager by Angela S Lucas", it is a great read for

.

anyone negotiating semi-retirement or retirement it is an inspiration, thank you Angela.[32] I began to marvel and wondered could this be the help that I now would need with my book to get it published. I am writing this with a smile on my face because Angela, after reading my book said "Jane I have read your book and am awestruck! Certainly it is for wider reading!" All praise to you my faithful Lord, my Savour and friend. Your will be done regarding this book.

[32] *Footnote: 'How to be a Super Ager' by Angela S Lucas can be purchased on Amazon.*

Chapter 32: Havens Christian Hospices

Well dear reader, I have to confess and as I explained at the beginning of the book, I put my book on the shelf and got on with my new job as a Healthcare Chaplain. And now after nine and a bit years, of loving my job, fulfilling work and meeting hundreds of beautiful souls, I had given my all and it was time to leave. But back in the early days, I quickly had to learn, the art of what I call, "study listening" and I remember I asked myself "what was the point of me, as Chaplain," in a place, where a lot of the time folk were heartbroken, in the early stages of bereavement or preparing for end of life and for the next life. I remember the learning curve was steep and probably one of the greatest challenges of my life.

As part of the Chaplaincy team our daily routine was to visit both Little Havens and Fair Havens patients to have a Chapel time and to visit our Day Care Hospice. During the chapel time at Little Havens there was a lot of blowing bubbles, loud and wonderful music, often with lots of actions, Dougie Dug was a favourite and the song "Our God is a Great Big God". For the young teens I had some Christian rap music but the popular song with staff and children was an updated trendy version of 'Oh happy day When Jesus washed my sins away'. We used lots of stickers, the little ones loved them and they loved lots of stories I had told over the many years. Sometimes, in the summer months we were outside in our beautiful gardens. Other times it could be at the bedside if a child was resting, in the chapel of course but it could be in the dining room, wet play area or multi-sensory room, it was all about the children being comfortable or where they were chilling. I am smiling typing this at the thought of it all. It was wonderful and so much fun and I loved it. One day I read a prayer to God that had been written by one of our children, it touched my heart and I wondered how God felt hearing it, it went something like "I may be little but my love for God is huge Amen". At Fair Havens chapel prayers we would often play a piece of music and give a scripture with a thought for the day or tell a story and we had very many special times with patients sometimes joining us. There were faithful staff who came together to pray for the patients and staff and I believe it made a world of difference. I felt early on in my work that God was and is in the corridors of the Hospices, his peace and hope and love are all around each day. I believe there is a very thin space between heaven and earth at the hospices, I mean by that, God is near, the hospices were God's vision and are in his view and heart at all times.

One of our special volunteers Tony, always said to me "you must write down your experiences and the journey you have been on at the hospices". So my wish is to give a glimpse through my ministry, in a sensitive and respectful way. There is always a sense in caring that you receive far more than you give on reflection. I was regularly inspired by our children and their mums and dads and by our patients.

I can only say, without God, there is totally no way that I could have done my job as a Chaplain, God was totally faithful to me. I would often think, here goes Lord 'I am on a wing and a prayer here' and God would enable me to walk and support others in very complex situations. I had to learn to walk compassionately, sensitively and to listen. I had to grasp what was really being said, and understand what were the feelings behind the words, in often critical situations. I've always been good in a crisis and I think this is my God given gift, sounds strange but that said I had always to be ready in my day and I did my best and I thank God with all my heart for being a part of Havens Hospices.

One day, I was chatting to one of our wonderful nurses and I was saying how amazing it was, that all people died in peace, because that was my experience at the hospices, in fact, it was my only experience of end of life. When Nurse Julie looked directly at me and said, "No Jane that's just the hospices". Specialist care, holistic care for the body, mind and spirit makes the real difference. For me, I can say that I have seen and known end of life as a beautiful experience for our families. People who are made comfortable and with their symptoms controlled at end of life while also surrounded by loved ones, these are beautiful moments of being together living every hour. The love you sense in the rooms is often tangible. "Making every day and moment count" is the Hospices motto and that's what all the staff aim for giving a hundred and ten percent effort for our families. I have undertaken many weddings and wedding blessings, they have been beautiful. I remember one young couple having a blessing. On the day they both dressed in their wedding outfits and their Mum gave her blessing to the couple. It was sacred and beautiful. Our nurses and fund raising team, time and again all would rally on such occasions, making rooms into wedding venues and arranging for wedding cakes and champagne to be served. A naming ceremony, in a home was very precious and so meaningful for the whole family. The criteria is that in the hospice baptisms or Christenings can only be offered if a child is at end of life.

Steve Nolan writes in his book *"Spiritual Care at the End of Life"* about being a Chaplain that it is all about being a "hopeful presence" and I like this description.[33] Hope in Palliative Care is vital, as hope is needed for living, without it humans survive only and don't live I believe. But you might say hope in death, but yes we all need hope in our dying phase. Well how? I can hear. This is something that I learnt by being around death every day. Hope whether it is in a basic belief that somehow love lives on in some form or other in the next life, phase or in heaven. As a Chaplain, when you introduce yourself there can be an instant trust given to you but it can for some people mean mistrust. Often people will talk and reflect at end of life about their life. As a Chaplain, its assessing how best you can offer support whilst respecting people's needs and dreams.

This was a revelation to me, that a person can find hope in death. I remember when I first got to the hospice I struggled with what was the help I could bring. Being a minister you are often talking a lot, but being a chaplain

---

[33] Footnote: Steve Nolan, the title *"The Chaplain as a 'Hopeful Presence"*, *Spiritual Care at the End of Life*, *(Jessica Kingsley Publishers, London, 2012)*

you have to be comfortable in quiet, painful moments and listen a whole lot. Yes there are sad times, and I remember one year where there was so many tears it seemed in the Chapel. But there is a lot of fun and laughter too in both hospices. Other than trying to get a smile from the children and young people each day, I also held to the aim that I must never get it wrong, no wrong words or clichés not ever wishing to add insult to already painful and difficult times. We have all felt the pain of a well-meaning friend with a cliché at hand. But I tried and learned rather to walk in gentleness, stripping away all assumptions and making no judgements, accepting folk and caring from all faith backgrounds or no faith. It was a privilege for me and a joy to relate in this way.

On visiting the In Patient Unit one morning I heard one patient say he really wanted to play a game of drafts. I let him know that I had the game at home and would bring it in. The next day there we were playing drafts, laughing together and he was chatting away and told me the story of his life. This dear man could not sleep, so I offered to return later and say a short prayer before bed, he said "yes" and later we prayed and he slept through.

On one visit, I met up with a nursing assistant and we were singing to a patient. In loose terms she was playing the guitar, and we were singing the song "I will walk ten thousand miles..." to a patient and then she launched into "Edelweiss..." from fun to a poignant song in a moment. Honestly, I do not know how she pulled it off, but she did and as we walked out of the patient's room, he said "love you" and straight back the nursing assistance replied, "we love you too". Wow, how funny and how moving situations can be when you're living in the moment.

Dame Cicely Saunders, *"The founder of the Modern Hospice Movement"*, said this was important;

> "Some will find it shocking that we should speak of accepting or even preparing for death and will think that both patient and doctor should believe in treatment and fight for life right up to the end. They may question how anyone should be satisfied with what sounds like such a negative role. To talk of accepting death when its approach has become inevitable is not mere resignation on the part of the patient nor defeatism or neglect on the part of the doctor. Certainly they will take no steps to hasten its coming, but for both of them it is the very

opposite of doing nothing. The patient may well achieve more in this part of his life than in any other, making of it a real reconciliation and fulfilment. This will do more than anything else to comfort the relative and help them on to the road to normal living again. Who is to say how far the effects may reach?" [34]

Working well as a palliative care team is vital, from team communication and balance of the right holistic care needed and tailored for each patient is a team effort. And as a team of staff we would be present in the heart break, being in the moments of the brutality of shocking death, when death comes it is always a shock whether or not your loved one had a short or long illness.

Daphne Hall MBE, co-founder of Havens Christian Hospices writes in *"Miracles that cannot be Counted"*;

[34] *Footnote: Cicely Saunders, "The Founder of the Modern Hospice Movement", Shirley du Boulay, p58-59 (Hodder & Stoughton, Great Britain, 2007)*

"During the years of involvement with dying people I was often asked how anyone could work constantly with people who were not going to get better, how could they cope with the negativity and hopelessness of that type of nursing. My answer was that it was not negative at all but for many nurses a wonderful way of expressing all the skills they had learned during their careers and gave them the opportunity to have time to care in a way that gave of themselves."

"A hospice, is not a place where people go to die, it is a place where they go to live until they die. Seen like this the time spent under 'hospice care' whether in a building or at home can be a positive experience for the patient and their family and friends. It can be a celebration of that person's life and be a time when families can store up positive memories. These can be brought out in their darkest days to encourage and support them."[35]

---

[35]*Footnote: Daphne Hall, MBE, "Miracles that Cannot be Counted", A History of Fair Havens Hospice, p29 (Local printer no details, 2003)*

I often used the quote to myself, "What Would Jesus Do?" It was really helpful and can give real insight. He would be there, caring, loving in a non-judgemental way. Try it.

On a home visit to a younger patient she asked me, if she would see her pets again in heaven? I explained my views and hope that she would be reunited and I shared the Rainbow Bridge poem with her and it seemed to give her great peace from then on. I would visit regularly and we would talk about the hard and difficult questions of life and eternal life but we would also laugh such precious memories I have. This dear patient showed such courage and arranged her whole funeral service and it was a service to remember and my total honour to lead. Courage and inspiration are what I've often seen in adversity.

I feel I've taken too many children's funerals, whilst at the same time being my very great privilege. In some ways, as you can imagine that is the saddest role and often after taking a baby's burial, the only way to describe my feelings that I needed to go and retreat to a forest and hide to recover. It is never right or fair, imagine the parents pain and sorrow. It is never right to see a Mum and Dad saying goodbye to their baby or child. I officiated at the funerals of lots of our children, babies and young adults. I feel that one day in heaven, I will meet all the lovely children again that I've prayed and cared for and what fun we will have together again. As staff we loved them and they loved us back, it was a beautiful thing. Again there is no making sense of it all, but my bottom line is if the hospices were not here the living hell that is lived out in these families lives would be far worse if we were not there at all.

One of the first days of working at Little Havens, I meet a young man playing pool and I asked if I could join him, with a twinkle in his eye he said yes and all I remember was that minutes later he won and slaughtered me at pool. I remember, when taking his funeral I took along the Little Havens pool cue as a prop to tell the story. I shall never forget him.

A remarkable faith one of our teenagers had in the face of such suffering. Every day she wanted chapel time and I remember walking in her room for our music and prayer time. On entering her room and saying hello, the nurse looked up at me and said 'Jane that is the first time we have had a smile today' I felt overwhelmed with a flood of feelings. When a soul is very poorly, you see the true spirit. This young soul showed us all such grit, such faith, such spirit and beauty in the face of being gravely ill and at end of life.

I have never worked with so many caring people as the staff at Havens and we all would keep an eye on each other, to make sure we all had support. That is how it worked in both hospices. The good news is that palliative care, treatments and medications and feeds have all improved over my time and Little Havens children are living longer with life limiting illnesses. Time is being given and greater quality of life has vastly improved for our adults and children. Thank heavens for our National Health Service and for those in it tirelessly working for good, God bless them.

My hope is that heaven will be a wonderful place, we get glimpses through the words in the Bible and on beautiful days here on earth. I remember one bereaved parent sat me down and asked me about Heaven, as a result I typed out some bible verses all about heaven and have included them.[36] A favourite Bible verse of

[36] *Footnote: Please see Appendix 1 Heaven Bible verses*

mine and often used for solace with patients who have faith or exploring and wanting to reach out in faith at end of life is found in Revelation. This passage offers real hope that our God has a plan for our lives and future;

> Then I saw a new heaven and a new earth, for the first heaven and the first earth had passed away, and there was no longer any sea. I saw the Holy City, the new Jerusalem, coming down out of heaven from God, prepared as a bride beautifully dressed for her husband. And I heard a loud voice from the throne saying, "Now the dwelling of God is with men, and he will live with them. They will be his people, and God himself will be with them and be their God. He will wipe every tear from their eyes. There will be no more death or mourning or crying or pain, for the old order of things has passed away." He who was seated on the throne said, "I am making everything new!" Then he said, "Write this down, for these words are trustworthy and true." He said to me: "It is done, I am the Alpha and the Omega, the Beginning and the End. To him who is thirsty I will give to drink without cost from the spring of the water of life. He who overcomes will inherit

all this, and I will be his God and he will be my child…"[37]

One day, I was called in to see a patient and asked if she would like a short prayer and she acknowledged me and nodded. I read Psalm 23 which seemed to give some comfort. I can't recommend this Psalm enough, it has eternal hope and comfort through its words somehow, and has comforted many people in my time. I sensed God was saying to me to sit by the bedside and continue to pray to myself which is what I did. Then after a time I left. The next day I went back to visit and noticed straight away that the patient was wearing a beautiful new, silver cross and chain. During the night, the patient asked the night nurse, "Could you do what Jane did?" and the nurse said 'what was that?' "As Jane prayed there was a warmth and a peace that moved down my whole body that I have never felt before?" For me, on hearing this, I knew that was God's Holy Spirit, giving heavenly peace, comfort and hope and the patient wanted some more, bless her.

[37] Footnote 34: NIV Bible, Revelation 21.1-7

Psalm 23

The Lord is my Shepherd,
I shall not be in want.
He makes me lie down in green pastures,
He leads me beside quiet waters,
He restores my soul.
He guides me in paths of righteousness for his
name's sake.
Even though I walk through the valley of the
shadow of death,
I will fear no evil, for you are with me;
Your rod and your staff,
They comfort me.
You prepare a table before me in the presence
of my enemies.
Your anoint my head with oil,
My cup overflows.
Surely goodness and love will follow me all the
days of my life,
And I will dwell in the house of the Lord for
ever.[38]

---

[38] Footnote: NIV Bible, Psalm 23

Spirituality

The Apostle Paul said "So now faith, hope and love abide, these three, but the greatest of these is love." [39] Keeping it simple and helping patients with Spiritual care, these three things are the only things that matter, for personal life, relationships and a faith for life and after life. Palliative care and spiritual care is enhanced where a little faith, even faith in love, a little hope and a lot of love and care are administered. I would like to outline some important spiritual needs and endeavour to talk about the complexities and struggles that there are at End of Life for people with Faith and without a Faith. Whilst faith in its loosest term simply means "faith in people," and where there is no belief system, faith in love is vitally needed; when hope is lost and you might say where is the hope at end of life? But hope is in the love shared at these often precious times when these painful symptoms are relieved. When death is coming and there is no belief system, hope can seem lost, and that there is no hope. At this time the patients can experience a total plan and it is totally painful and can manifest in spiritual and emotional pain adding to the already chronic physical symptoms. So what forms

[39] Footnote: ESV, Holy bible, 1 Corinthians 13.10

of hope are there at end of life? Living in the moment sharing company of loved ones, a smile, holding hands, enjoying music, a cream tea with a friend, a marriage proposal and wedding to your life long partner, often just in the nick of time, all these times add meaning in sharing with loved ones. On the other hand, I would say generally where there is a simple, dare I say primal basic belief system, in living on in the next world, a simple faith in God and heaven, for the dying soul it can bring great peace, at end of life. Also in the extreme, I have seen "Anger" another emotion when people don't wish to die yet, perhaps a younger adult, which is very sad to see and it is their way and they are dying their way and that is completely understandable. I have seen people turn their heads to the wall, turning away from life and having had enough. Also for the families who have seen their loved one suffer, there can be a relief of sorts that their loved one, in death, suffers no more. In contrast, I have seen the young at peace and having acceptance at their end of life. Over the years I have met many people who said their prayers at night, but did not go to church and I would say that seventy percent of people had this faith when I started out in my work, but I did see a decline over the decade.

A man's family approached the Chaplaincy department one day, desperately asking for help for their loved one.

The patient was approaching end of life and was anxious, fearful and could not settle. I remember entering the room, saying a swift prayer on the way. The conversation I had with the man, wife and daughter, was briefly to outline the patient did not have a faith but he was feeling uneasy and experiencing some anguish. I noticed and remarked that I could sense a lot of love in the room, I said "could it be possible to believe that your love for one another will not end and somehow you will be altogether one day in your love?" I asked if I could read a poem by Mary Hollingsworth and after this the patient seemed to have some peace and be more settled:

> Love is stronger than death.
> So I must be content to know that
> love is not affected by death--
> it doesn't end, it doesn't diminish,
> it doesn't change.
> Instead, love is immortalized
> and eternalized through death.
> And the possibility of that love ever
> being damaged or broken
> is eliminated forever.
> I'll put my trust in love.[40]

[40] Footnote: Read more at
http://www.beliefnet.com/prayers/christian/death/love-is-stronger-than-death.aspx#uuSSRmSSxKwVrMzg.99

Peace is the ultimate goal, it's what the family wants to feel and certainly what the staff aim for. Spirituality is the essence of a person. It is the thing that gives meaning to a life. If we have no peace in our hearts or minds when facing death it is a desperate state of affairs and it was my role and in some ways I have often felt like a mid-wife, a spiritual mid-wife, helping people at end of life, to find peace and hope. Somehow with God's help I have been used to ease spiritual pain and work towards spiritual peace at end of life. Even in my ministry on Canvey I could see it and I truly believe that if we don't look after our spiritual health each day, walking in the fields, finding peace by a river or sea, listening to the birds, those sorts of thing then I believe that depression can be today's by product of that.

Faith

It often seemed over the years that many of our patients did pray regularly. It is a common known fact that when people are facing a trauma or emergency that is life threatening people do turn to God in prayer. I would say that for over half of our patients prayer was important and part of their spirituality. Along with the

Psalm 23, The Lord 's Prayer, from Matthew, Chapter 6 is also comforting at end of life. For example, both talk about a spiritual life living on, "I shall dwell in the house of the Lord forever" "Father who art in heaven… thy will be done, forgive us and help us to forgive those who have sinned against us… deliver me from evil, power for ever and ever." These texts are so reassuring at end of life and something with a firm foundation to hang on to. I myself had a spiritual need when having severe pneumonia and whilst on life support would try to recite Psalm 23 in my mind, it was difficult but I kept on and it helped me. I believe at end of life, our spiritual selves feel very much more vital and real and in touch with the God's deep love, our maker and creator, in my experience.

A patient who was an atheist came to the hospice for care and I was not visiting them, as requested. Then one day the night nurse approached me and said the lady would like to see me. It was early in the morning when I went into the room. On approaching the bedside, I sat there and explained that the night nurse had said she would like a visit. We just sat for a bit and the lady gave one big, loud scream. I felt that I should stay put, I was thinking the scream, a scream of frustration, or some physical pain or physiological pain? My intuition told me that somehow it was my test. Now isn't intuition a wonderful thing. Our whole bodies are in tune with another soul, we are being with them and can sense things. These things are truths and guide us, many of our palliative care team had great intuition and I think for end of life, it is certainly another sense, and a precious skill to listen too. I asked the lady if she would like me to say a short prayer asking for peace and she said "yes". Each day I went in to visit and said a short prayer and read Psalm 23, and the lady seemed to experience a sense of peace.

I find stories are the very best way of understanding spiritual concepts and dynamics. The first time I heard mentioned the term Spiritual pain, I was intrigued but witnessing it first-hand can truly say that it is an unbearable state of being for any human. It is the total absence of peace. The other difficult thing that is for every human there is a unique key to getting the soul to a place of being settled in one's self, and it takes as long as it takes too. There was a man I had met in our Day Care Hospice and who I had got to know over some time, I remember he was a Darwinist in his views and whilst initially he had put his hands up, in front of me, in defence from me, as the Chaplain, I instantly said I would love to hear his point of view, as I was very interested. In no time we soon understood each other and shared easily. On one day the Junior Doctor came in to the chaplaincy office and said could I help, explaining a patient was refusing to eat. Unsure about precisely what I could do, I said a prayer to myself to God, as I walked to the patient's room. On entering the room the patient recognised me and welcome me to sit, I sat and listened and listened some more, as the patient chatted, occasionally I reflected the feelings I sensed he was experiencing, to see if I had understood him correctly and gently clarified what he was saying to me. Then all of a sudden after about twenty minutes, he said "Oh well I think I had better have something to eat then!" Just like that, my thoughts are I think he had an emotional blockage, he needed to share and be understood and literally get his thoughts off his chest. This needed to happen to literally make room for food. You know yourself if there is something you are anxious about the last thing you fancy is food and how when we can talk to a best friend about a trouble we feel better once we have shared. The old saying is true a problem shared is a problem halved. I am not saying there is always a quick result like this to psychological pain being suffered.

Walking with Mums and the whole family when a baby has suddenly died is probably the hardest thing I have ever done. I remember sitting on the carpet while a Mum let her pain, shock and sorrow out. I remember the time I had with a mum and dad and sister all grieving in one room and how I had to identify and give value to the different types of grieving with a family, to make them unified and together. Often women will want to sit in a dark room and cry and men to go off and do something, some kind of occupation because men and women do grieve differently on the whole. The woman can feel polarized in her grief and that the man is not grieving. By just pointing out the two types of grieving, generally speaking, helps a little in the very painful process of the bereavement of a child.

As you can imagine, it is not easy to walk with families whose baby has suddenly died or to be along young parents traumatised by their child's illness, but at such times I have seen and experienced such precious, intimate moments and parents who are totally inspirational in their love and care. But it is the greatest privilege when a family ask you to join them at this precious time, and at the hospice it is a beautiful thing to have a grieving suite, where there is time where parents can hold the hand of their deceased baby, child and teenager. A time to come, to cope with the great grief, pain and loss, as we all know it is not the way life should be, for a child to die before their parent. It is a primal thing and time is given and time is needed for the stages of grief to be lived through. With the wonderful sensitive staff at hand and just when needed if end of life is managed with great care, pain is managed physically and spiritually, then end of life can be beautiful. Let me try to explain, it is like the beginning of life at end of life being surrounded by your loved ones, with all the love in the world around you, times still to exchange a smile or an I love you, or maybe holding a hand. In this way memories are made that seem eternal and that you never forget. It is a time of saying "Good Bye". Most people are glad when they sit in with their loved ones, but it takes courage.

Another thing in my experience is that people die better when they do have some sort of afterlife belief system. Achieving the goal of inner peace can be achieved more easily. Why? As we have reflected, space and time in a caring space is needed. Being willing to hear and see what is needed at end of life is a subtle getting it right for each family.

As a Spiritual Care Giver, it is important to know your own limits of care giving, there have only been a handful of times over the years, when I have met patients with whom I did not connect. Thank heavens. The reason, was not always obvious. A chemistry? I do not know, or maybe I reminded them of someone or maybe they reminded me of someone. The dynamics were complex. It is certainly true that in life we click with people, but on a few occasions we don't. There is an answer. We are a Chaplaincy team and it is important to skilfully work together and let other Chaplains support patients that they had connected with and that is how we worked together. At these times of offering support and to befriend and to be with the patients in their journey. One thing is for sure, none of us are indispensable, and I wasn't. But when you think we were seeing over a thousand patients including their families a year, the important thing is to dove-tale the service, and, to work all together as a team for the very best outcomes. Thank you wonderful Chaplaincy team, I often said we were a family of sorts working together and the work itself was a great privilege but so was working all together, may God continue to bless you and Havens Hospices.

Young children can go to the brink of death then come back to living so often and it is harrowing to sense the roller coaster of emotions that take a family to its limits. But even so I have been inspired to see how families keep on going and continue somehow for another extra mile, day, after day.

The concepts of spirituality and care at end of life is diverse and complex, but I hope in the sharing it will enable you, as you support people in your life who are grieving.

Spiritual Care for those of all faiths and none

In the hospice world a well used phrase and aim is that "we care for all people of all faiths or of no faith". To accept all people regardless of background, creed or nationality is vitally important. And in a sense brings hope and acceptance for all. Can a chaplain truly provide this? We had some photo books as a resource for patients that could no longer speak or were too poorly and I would often sit and go through a photo book with them. One of them was black and white photos from the past, the other book was based on family life. It was a way of communicating and helping patients to be distracted for a moment and maybe to remember childhood or family times in the past. It was quite powerful. I remember, I even had a gentleman buy these books for his loved one in the hospice because they enjoyed them together so much. Reminiscing and remembering are important at end of life. It is very powerful.

So how do we decide what gives meaning to our lives? For most of us being with the family is key. It can also be types of music, walking in the countryside, experiencing the elements sunshine and the wind, many patients will strive to make it down to the Hospice garden regularly or even to the seafront which is only 300 yards away. Spiritual care is something that adds to your experience of living.

For a Muslim patient who needed the Quran read to him, it brought a peace. I remember I found some Abraham texts to read and that it helped. I placed a simple marker in the page and a night nurse continued the reading at night I found out later. That's great team work.

Many are the chats with a chaplain from a life story shared, what an honour that is; to forgiveness explored for another and the liberating feeling that is to forgive another who has caused you hurt. Confession, at end of life there sometimes is a need to go through the detail of life more fully a type of confessing truths. I have known many patients when I have asked what was their favourite holiday, will often in the telling, re live happy memories or if asked to talk about a grandchild, the emotions are drawn from the memory bank and can be realised again. This is a lovely exercise that I have often repeated with patients over the years.

For some patients spiritual care contains faith and for others is does not, but everyone has a spiritual dimension, it is that simple and the important thing is to be accepted for who we are and that the things in life that bring meaning to us are diverse and broad and very important. I have added some spiritual care questions at the back of the book to help.[41]

[41] *Footnote: A help list of questions is enclosed in the Appendix: Questions from Australia, Steinhauser*

Chapter 33: Chelmsford Cathedral Centenary

At the recent meeting of the Chelmsford Diocese Healthcare Chaplains meeting it had been hinted that there would be a very important person attending the Centenary celebrations of the Diocese and Cathedral. It had also been hinted that some of the Healthcare Chaplains would be invited on behalf of the people they represented in the community. Wow, this was exciting.

I was sort of waiting for the post to arrive, with excitement and it did. A golden ticket literally it read, written in gold;

A service of celebration to mark

The centenary of the Diocese of Chelmsford and Chelmsford Cathedral

In the presence of Her Majesty The Queen and His Royal Highness the Duke of Edinburgh

On Tuesday 6 May 2014

At Chelmsford Cathedral

As I read the card invitation I was literally bouncing round the house with excitement. Oh my, how excited I was, it was off the richter scale, you can only imagine. I hadn't bought a new suit since my graduation and it was high time to get a new one, I bought a silver grey suit and wore my pink clerical shirt for the occasion.

The big day came and it was amazing, it was a sunny day it was time to go into the Cathedral. You had to take with you your ticket and passport to enter the Cathedral and on walking up to the Cathedral a police constable said "Good Morning Ma'am" to me, as I entered.

We were all seated, I was with our CEO Andy Smith and there was a real buzz in the air and the great and the good collected inside and outside the Cathedral. The time came and suddenly we heard a great cheer outside, we all knew that her Majesty and the Duke had arrived. The Cathedral for that Ceremony had all the seats turned in to the aisle. The sun shone through the top windows of the Cathedral as the Queen and Duke walked down the aisle, the Queen was wearing cream and she looked beautiful and as the sun shone down she looked resplendent, I will never forget. The cathedral looked stunning, flowers everywhere. I was seated about twenty five feet away from the Queen it was amazing, they sat on special throne like seats. We sang;

"All people that on earth do dwell, sing to the Lord with cheerful voice; him serve with fear, his praise forth tell, come ye before him, and rejoice:" "Now thank we all our God with hearts and hands and voices who wondrous things hath done, in whom his world rejoices:" "God save our gracious Queen, long live our noble Queen, God save the Queen. Send her victorious, happy and glorious, long to reign over us: God Save the Queen."

Each of us received a lovely A4 size order of service. The Right Reverend Stephen Cottrell, The Lord Bishop of Chelmsford preached and said something like, "we were all there to represent the people that we served on this very special day", it was inspirational and an honour to be representing Havens Hospice's families. It is quite special to sing God Save the Queen to the Queen, it was a total blessing and as the Queen walked out at the end of the ceremony, I curtseyed to show my great respect and gratitude. And the organist was playing the *"Organ Voluntary"*, triumphantly. I often pray for the Queen and the Government, but never did I think I would be present to worship God with the Queen of England, United Kingdom. Praise God.

The next day, I was also invited to attend a seminar taken by the Bishop of Canterbury Justin Welby and was introduced afterwards. It was all amazing and a heavenly blessing.

Thank you friends at the Cathedral for the invites, may God continue to richly bless you now and in the years to come.

Chapter 34: 2016

In 2016, I was diagnosed with stage three breast cancer, I had surgery followed by chemotherapy. It was shocking to get the news and I took three weeks to get my head around it and I kept calm and carried on working, like some do. I love the saying, "keep calm and carry on", it helps and comes of course from the World War II years, as we all know but the saying can help us too in our personal wars today, I believe. Truly the inspiration in my life, are my dear Mum and Dad, both survivors of the London Blitz, they both lost close family members, my Dad was buried alive with his family and his Mother, Father and Sister Ellen all died, God rest their dear souls, how did Dad survive that! My Mum was in school and heard a bomb and they all ran outside and my Mum saw her house had been hit and her Mother, Nanny Dickens and Aunty Jessie and her toddler Malcolm and baby James all died, may God hold them in His eternal love and care. I recently said to Mum, "I don't know how you and Dad managed after all that sadness to get up again and go on" and my Mum said "you didn't have any choice you just had too." I said "one day you will be with them all again Mum and then forever" and that is what we hope for. So I kept calm and I carried on working, trying to come to terms with my new diagnosis. The surgery was planned and I worked up to it and then went off and had Chemo too.

I was fortunate with my Chemo and the staff at Southend Chemotherapy unit were amazing and my Surgeon saved my life. I feel and I will always be eternally grateful for taking away the cancer. And probably because I had been used to helping poorly children and adults over many years, I understood how best to managed high temperatures and had inside information. I did all the things I needed to do such as plenty of hydration, managing with fans and cool flannels and ice lollies and crushed ice the journey through Chemotherapy. The importance of eating little and often, I got through it all, and with no doubt the many prayers of many friends at the hospices and home, rooting for me and two weeks after my last Chemo session, I was back at work with a wig on and plasters keeping my finger nails in place.

Getting back to work was so important to me and I am so grateful to Havens for supporting me through it all, they were very kind to me. When you are wearing a wig, the only problem is it changes your sense of coordination and one day I missed the first step on the stairs at Fair Havens and my wig and I nearly parted. On another occasion at the BP garage at Rayleigh, a gust of wind took my wig straight off and you never see me move so fast and I whipped my hood on and pick up my wig as fast as I could, interesting CCTV that made I bet. I think however, and hope that my experience helped me over the next two years of hospice work to understand more fully, treatment suffering and maybe something good came out of my suffering.

Something Good out of Something Bad

The only thing that I cling on to is that what God does do for us He can take our bad situations and bring out some good from them. What a wonder that is, something good out of something bad happening. God doesn't always take away the difficulties in our lives, but he will put you in the path of just the right person or help at the right time. Or how blessed I am for my life to be in the time line of the NHS, they have saved me again and again and I am very grateful.

A loved one once asked me "did God make bad things happen?" Immediately I said "No, God does not make the bad things come to us, but he will help us and does love us and prayer can lead to peace and hope in the situation."

He sustains us in our trials and sorrows, I am often comforted by Jesus words;

"In this world you will have trouble. But take heart! I have overcome the world."[42] Good news, we are not alone. Also my heartfelt thanks to my dear Sis in law Tracey for all your love and help. Thank God for Family.

[42] *Footnote: NIV Bible John 16.33*

Chapter 35: Another Special Service

My good friend and my best Boss ever, former Head of Care at Havens Hospices, Catherine Wood RN, usually attended a service to commemorate Florence Nightingale and had VIP tickets and invited me along to Westminster Abbey.

As we walked in to the Abbey, two red coated Chelsea Pensioners said "good evening girls", well that was lovely on all counts, being called a girl and meeting them there. Smiling, we walked down the side aisle to the front and were seated by OBE awarded stewards wearing their OBEs. We were sitting twenty feet away from the royal dignitary and again the seats were facing in to the aisle. The organ was amazing, at the Abbey and again a little bit of heaven on earth. We sang;

"Praise to the Lord, the Almighty, the King of Creation"; "Be Thou My Vision; "I Vow to Thee, My Country"; "Guide me, O Thou Great Redeemer" and "God Save Our Gracious Queen".

At the end we pondered the Life of Florence Nightingale and her legacy to our generation and many testimonies from many nurses were given, it was a very special evening.

Westminster Abbey

A Service to Commemorate the Life of Florence Nightingale

Wednesday 17th May 2017, at 6.30pm

Entrance Great West Door. Dr John Hall Dean

After the service we were walking out past the two lady Generals and down the aisle and I said to my friend; "Catherine, just imagine who has walked down this aisle" and Catherine not missing a beat said "Jane, Kings and Queens my friend, Kings and Queens." As we got outside the bells were ringing and it was raining, what a blessing I felt to be worshipping in the Abbey and to come outside and the bells be ringing so magnificently I shall never forgot that evening. Thank you God and thank you Catherine.

We then got a cab and went for tea at the Tower Hotel. It was a perfect end to the evening.

Chapter 36: And finally Grandchildren

My God and my surgeon have got me to see my two
stunningly beautiful grandchildren, never in a million
years did I ever think I would be a Nanny. People don't
tell you that you will fall in love with your grandchildren,
I am totally head over tails in love again, this time with
two tiny beauties Lily-Mae Guest and Ava-Rose Guest,
my heaven sent joys and shining lights in my life.

I am now busy being a Nanny, things that dreams are
made of that's for sure and spending a bit more time
with my Mum and Dad, this is our time.

John 10:10 our Havens Hospices verse Jesus said "I have
come that you may have life and have it to the full." We
are building a New Fair Havens Hospice with no stairs
for the patients to get up and down, praise God. It will
be completed in 2020, a much needed purpose built
New Adult Hospice with Sixteen Beds. I believe God
helps us in our troubles and the hospices are a beautiful
reflection of His love and care for all people. "Our God,
He is an ever present help in times of trouble."[43]

---

[43] Footnote: NIB Bible, Psalm 46.1

May God bless and keep you and yours, may he guide you to His eternal Hope for life and eternal life. Thank you for reading my book and making every book count.

Epilogue

Of course there have many more experiences of life unwritten, but my wish for this book is that it will help the reader find their destiny in the middle of broken dreams and find healing through the love God has just for them. Don't leave it, get yourself enrolled on the next Alpha Course near you, you won't regret it.

I just know this to be loved and to love with all your heart, the most high God, is most worthy of pursuits and I love my God, my Father, my Jesus and precious Holy Spirit, I could not live without them. And to love the ones He gives to you, with all your heart and soul. One day there will be an incredible encounter when I will see my precious God face to face and the rainbows and dreams will be even more joyous and vivid there than anything that has gone before here. I hope you have been inspired, helped or comforted. God is a prayer away, he will answer you, be open and sincere in your prayer. I would like to end with these words of a song that have often moved me and inspired me. The Song helps us to look upwards and find hope for our days. May you know God's love for you and may he continue to bless you in your life now and forever.

God will make a way
Where there seems to be no way
He works in ways we cannot see
He will make a way for me.
He will be my guide, hold me closely to his side
With love and strength for each new day
He will make a way, God will make a way.

By a roadway in the wilderness he'll lead me
Rivers in the desert will I see
Heaven and earth will fade but his word will still
remain
He will do something new today

Don Moen 1997

Appendix 1

Heaven

Genesis Chapter 28, verses 12 & 17
'In a dream he saw a stairway standing on the earth. Its
top reached to heaven. The angels of God were going
up and coming down on it. The Lord stood above the
stairway. He said, 'I am the Lord. I am the God of your
grandfather Abraham and the God of Isaac. I will give
you and your children after you the land on which you
are lying... I am with you. I will watch over you
everywhere you go.'

Matthew Chapter 5, verses 3-10
Jesus said 'Blessed are those who are sad, for theirs is
the kingdom of heaven. Blessed are those who mourn
for they will be comforted... Blessed are the pure in
heart, for they will see God... Rejoice and be glad,
because great is your reward in heaven...'

Matthew Chapter 22, verse 30, 32
Jesus said, about those who have died 'At the
resurrection people ...will be like the angels in heaven...
He is not the God of the dead but of the living.'

Luke Chapter 23, verse 39-43

The robber's conversation who was crucified with Jesus, gives an extraordinary insight to heaven.

One of the criminals who hung there hurled insults at Jesus, "Aren't you the Christ? Save yourself and us!" But the other criminal rebuked him. "Don't you fear God?," he said, "since you are under the same sentence? We are punished justly, and are getting what our deeds deserve. But this man has done nothing wrong." Then he said, "Jesus, remember me when you come into your Kingdom." Jesus answered him, "I tell you the truth, today you will be with me in paradise."

My thoughts on the above passages

They bring a wonderful hope that with God the Christian faith teaches we are to go on living, our spirits will live on after our earthly bodies die, in fact we will have a new body like Christ's risen body, so exciting and a hope story to change the world that's for sure. For example, I believe with all my heart that one day, me and my family will be altogether in God's glorious kingdom which is for everybody. I love this verse and the message is simple God loves all he has made. Psalm 145 verse 9. In my experience the majority of souls believe and I think it is a primal hope that one day, in some way they will be reunited with their loved ones who have died. It's all about a little hope, faith and lots of love.

John chapter 3, verse 16 "For God so loved the world that he gave his only begotten Son, that whoever believes in him shall not perish but have eternal life." God does not make his love difficult to find, it's beautiful and it's attractive, it's not about attending Church, but I personally love to meet with others and celebrate my God, but the truth is He just loves you and is a prayer away. I think a large percentage of people pray when they are facing bereavement or at end of life, there is a special, sacred perceptive at this time of our lives. And as humans we must respect all people's decisions at such a time. Some people are angry when dying, but I have to say they are few, I am grateful for that, they are going too soon and they are angry, it is tragic and a mystery. But most souls come to peace and serenity at end of life here on earth.

For me there is a day to be born and a day to die, King Solomon tells us, both are precious days and sacred and beautiful. It does not seem fair and on such days, when the days are hellish, because of a death, that seems too soon, I think that if the hospices were not here it would be a whole lot more hellish, that is a very basic truth to hold on to. The hospices are the provision of God's love and He is near but it is so hard though. Tragically some bodies cannot sustain life anymore and that is a great tragedy for a family, but we will walk with them always.

I Corinthians 15:53-58

The Apostle Paul wrote and quotes the Old Testament, "For the perishable must clothe itself with the imperishable, and the mortal with immortality. When the perishable has been clothed with the imperishable and the mortal with immortality, then the saying that is written will come true:" "Death has been swallowed up in victory."

"Where O death, is your victory? Where, O death, is your sting?"

The sting of death is sin, and the power of sin is the law. But thanks be to God! He gives us the victory through our Lord Jesus Christ.

For faith exploration I recommend the Alpha course.

Kübler-Ross model

Stages of grief in terminal illness

The stages, popularly known by the acronym DABDA, include:[6]

1. **Denial** – The first reaction is denial. In this stage, individuals believe the diagnosis is somehow mistaken, and cling to a false, preferable reality.

2. **Anger** – When the individual recognizes that denial cannot continue, they become frustrated, especially at proximate individuals. Certain psychological responses of a person undergoing this phase would be: "Why me? It's not fair!"; "How can this happen to me?"; "Who is to blame?"; "Why would this happen?".

3. **Bargaining** – The third stage involves the hope that the individual can avoid a cause of grief. Usually, the negotiation for an extended life is made in exchange for a reformed lifestyle. People facing less serious trauma can bargain or seek compromise. Examples include the terminally ill person who "negotiates with God" to attend a daughter's wedding or an attempt to bargain for more

time to live in exchange for a reformed lifestyle.

4. **Depression** – "I'm so sad, why bother with anything?"; "I'm going to die soon, so what's the point?"; "I miss my loved one; why go on?"
   During the fourth stage, the individual despairs at the recognition of their mortality. In this state, the individual may become silent, refuse visitors and spend much of the time mournful and sullen.

5. **Acceptance** – "It's going to be okay."; "I can't fight it; I may as well prepare for it."
   In this last stage, individuals embrace mortality or inevitable future, or that of a loved one, or other tragic event. People dying may precede the survivors in this state, which typically comes with a calm, retrospective view for the individual, and a stable condition of emotions.

In a book co-authored with David Kessler and published posthumously, Kübler-Ross expanded her model to include any form of personal loss, such as the death of a loved one, the loss of a job or income, major rejection, the end of a relationship or divorce, drug addiction, incarceration, the onset of a disease or an infertility diagnosis, and even minor losses, such as a loss of insurance coverage.[4]

Kübler-Ross model

From Wikipedia, the free encyclopaedia

Appendix 3

Rainbow Bridge – Author Unknown
There is a bridge connecting Heaven and Earth,
It is called the Rainbow Bridge because of all its beautiful colours.
Just this side of the Rainbow Bridge there is a land of meadows,
Hills and valleys with lush green grass.
When a beloved pet dies, the pet goes to this place.
There is always food and water and warm spring weather.
The old and frail animals are young again.
Those who were sick, hurt or in pain are made whole again.
There is only one thing missing,
They are not with their special person who loved them so much on earth.
So each day they run and play until the day comes
When one suddenly stops playing and looks up!
The nose twitches! The ears are up!
The eyes are staring and this one runs from the group!
You have been seen and when you and your special friend meet,
You take him in your arms and hug him.
He licks and kisses your face again and again –
And you look once more into the eyes of your best friend and trusting pet.
Then you cross the Rainbow Bridge together never again to be apart.

Appendix 4

I felt I should share some reflections, these are some of the past Havens Hospices prayer diary back pages that I have written, May God bless you.

<u>Prayer diary No 1</u>

Imagination: makes the dullest day brighter
There: are times when it is enough to simply be
Those: who hold out a hand can reach for the stars
Laugh: and listen – especially to your heart
Excitement: is like bubbles in your heart
Happiness: is in the innocence of childhood
Appreciation: Enriches life
Value: all for who they are
Encouragement: makes us all better people
Nothing is impossible for those with dreams

A good colleague, Annie Spelling and friend dressed out Little Havens Chapel with these words and I wrote them down some time ago for my own use. Today I share them with you and please use them for your own meditation, sit and read through and explore.

Have you ever been away on holiday and for whatever reason you and your family start laughing over what seems the, silliest of things, but then a giggle turns into a belly laugh, too few times I feel we experience these spirit lifting and dare I say healing moments.

Furthermore, do you think our Lord Jesus had these moments with his disciples in the three years they travelled and ministered together?

So maybe it's been far too long since you experienced this kind of laughter and healing, or maybe you have been through a difficult time of bereavement or illness, my prayer for you today may God bless you with these words and bless you with unexpected laughter, the kind which is good for the soul.

God bless

Jane

<u>Prayer diary 2</u>

The Roman Catholic Church announced the Sainthood of Mother Teresa recently. What a beautiful soul; example of faith; humility; wisdom. Through hard work and loving those in great need around her these virtues that marked out a life of service in India.

Saint Mother Teresa said 'People are often unreasonable and self-centred. Forgive them anyway.
If you are kind, people may accuse you of ulterior motives. Be kind anyway.
If you are honest, people may cheat you. Be honest anyway.
If you find happiness, people may be jealous. Be happy anyway.
The good you do today may be forgotten tomorrow. Do good anyway.
Give the world the best you have and it may never be enough. Give your best anyway.
For you see, in the end, it is between you and God. It was never between you and them anyway.'
Footnote: www.goodreads

Wow... something for us to meditate on that dear friends and I sense a liberation from many shackles such as expectation and exhaustion from trying. Be yourself and soar... none of us are perfect but surely carving out a little freedom time for You will colour your whole life and enthuse you further to achieve more, not because the brain drain of 'ought' lead you about but because the kingdom secret of God's love poured over you in liberation and truth and you're making a splash being YOU noting the above. Thank you Saint Teresa and Thank you Lord Jesus that you will use these words to impact our lives today and as we move forward into tomorrow.

Jane

Prayer diary No 3

'Teacher... Teach me more. Speak to me of the secret of happiness, of health and hope, love and laughter. Instruct me in the way of peace, patience, gentleness, generosity and life-giving relationships. And show me how to conquer anger, envy, pride and despair. Make me wise.'

What a wonderful prayer Revd Nick Fawcett writes... from his new book *"The Teacher, A simple guide to daily life."*

Can you echo this prayer? It sums up just about the whole of the human experience! I love it. Spiritually it has it all and just reading it feels life-giving to me.

In the New Testament Paul speaks of the fruits of the Holy Spirit gentleness, kindness, patience.

Again something life giving to the human spirit.

If we seek to be more like Jesus and do strive to do what he would do I believe we will become more like him and exhibit these beautiful spiritual qualities.

For 13 years I have been staring at a boat on each dog walk that I have gone on with Rosie, my Dalmatian, the boat has challenged me in the seasons of life, its name is 'Patience' and isn't it true, in the fullness of God's timing our dreams and visions have each been fulfilled with a little patience.

God bless

Jane

Prayer Diary No 4

Then Jesus said to his disciples, 'If anyone would come after me, he must deny himself and take up his cross and follow me. For whoever wants to save his life will lose it, but whoever loses his life for me will find it. Matthew 16:24-26

In 2016, I underwent a period of ill health and an enforced rest and vigorous treatment was pursued, during which time this verse became by bottom line. I recently shared the notice of carrying our crosses in our lives. Whatever you are facing today if it be suffering physically, mentally and emotionally or all of the above, the bottom line is taking up our crosses and following Christ.

There is a sense of when facing the most difficult circumstances there is a way of tackling it that can be life giving to our bones, hearts and souls. God speaks to us at such times and will be right by your side. Timothy said, "...everyone had deserted me... But the Lord stood at my side and gave me strength..." 2 Timothy 4.16-17. We may not be facing Golgotha and the Roman cross but our choices, dilemma's and sufferings can be debilitating but even at such times it is important to do the little things keeping our hands busy like doing that craft that you are too busy working to try out...

formulating thoughts and life, trying to fathom it all, writing journals... making those double choc cookies for the teenagers to enjoy!

I met a friend who was also struggling with the limitations and frustrations of physical illness and I can only say we carry our crosses, it's not fair no, but illness comes and during which time our Lord is with us, in fact by our side.   And our hope and future days are in him. Should we as Christians suffer, well Jesus never promised us a rose garden, and said "...In this world you will have trouble. But take heart! I have overcome the world."   John 16.33 That is the key not to fear – it takes courage to choose not to live in fear with limiting facts, but live each day and keep going and keep on living by faith and hope.   As Christians we have a destination of heaven and boy is it going to be good.

One of my favourite films *"My Best Friend's wedding"* with Julia Roberts where she is struggling with her actions as a love sick friend and the porter tells her "this too shall pass." Great advice and I have often used it.

Carrying our crosses, is an action that will pass. There are blessings in these times spending quality times with family and friends that never would have happened. People showing their love to us by expressing good wishes, love in cards, flowers and presents sent to us, which we can thank God for.

After six months of chemotherapy approaching the last cycle felt that I was exiting the fight for life and entering life again and it felt good. Time to celebrate and live on. As I look forward I choose to live each day to the full and keep on keeping on doing good, where I can and helping to tell the Good News message of hope, faith and the love of God.

Prayer diary No 5

A dear friend sent me this text whilst I was recuperating after an operation and I found it really helpful, it is a notion that I have often contemplated but this is nicely put, the thought that the sky is blue far up above, when soaring in an aeroplane up through the grey clouds, up, up in to the blue sky it wonderful, to witness a sun rise up there is heavenly. My prayer for you may it bless you in your own situation today:

> Although the sky looks black,
> We know the sun is always there;
> And we can never be beyond our heavenly Father's care.
> Look up beyond the cloudy sky and see the sun above,
> Then rest assured we cannot be lost from the Father's love.

Amen. God bless you

Jane

Prayer Diary No 6

The Golden Nugget

When I was a kid we had a breakfast cereal called "Golden Grahams" which were little balls of golden nuggets and I loved to eat them before school. Little gold balls which soaked up the milk and were yummy. As a child, I loved golden nuggets but they are different for me now they are too sweet. For me now Golden Nuggets are God given "pearls of wisdom or revelation" and here is one for you today:

> "The lesson I have learnt is this, where lives lie broken and despair hangs heavy, never seek to give answers; give rather of yourself. Your time, your love, your care- for where life has lost its spark, we can only gently fan the smouldering embers until the flame ignites once more..."
> *Revd Nick Fawcett: "The Teacher, A Simple Guide to Daily Life," p31 (Kevin Mayhew, Croydon ,2016)*

A beautiful bible verse: Ps 30.5 "weeping may remain for a night, but rejoicing comes in the morning." Tears need to come and tears need to go...

I hope this gives guidance to those who would seek to support and hope to those in the valley of tears.

God bless you,   Jane

Appendix 5

Here are some Spiritual care questions that might be helpful:

Questions from Australia - Preparation and life completion intervention questions Steinhauser et al 2008

'Life story
Tell me about your life
What are your cherished times?
Of what are you most proud?
If someone were to make a movie of your life what would be important to include?
Forgiveness
If you were to do things again, what might you do differently?
Are there things or times you regret?
Is there anyone to whom you would like to offer forgiveness?
Is there anyone from whom you would like to ask forgiveness?
Are you at peace?
Heritage and legacy
What are your most valuable lessons learned?
What would you like to share with future generations? If you could choose one thing to pass on as your legacy what would that be?
What things would you like to accomplish?

BIBLIOGRAPHY

New International Version Holy Bible, (*The Gideons International, Lutterworth, England, 2002*)

Oxford NIV Scofield Study Bible, ed C I Scofield, (*Oxford University Press, 1984*)

English Standard Version, Holy Bible (*Crossway Publishing, China 2007*)

Eugene H Peterson, The Message, (*Alive Communications Inc, United States of Amercia,2002*) 'Scripture taken from the Message Copyright 2002, Used by permission of NavPress Publishing Group'

The Lion Handbook to the Bible, (*Lion Publishing, Malaysia, 1988*)

Fiona Castle, OBE, Forward (*Permissions given 2019*)

Daphne Hall, OBE, Miracles that Cannot be Counted, A History of Fair Havens Hospice, (*Local printer no details, 2003)*

Steve Nolan, Spiriutal Care at the End of Life, (*Jessica Kingsley Publishers, London, 2012*)

Cicely Saunders, The Founder of the Modern Hospice Movement, Shirley du Boulay, (*Hodder & Stoughton, Great Britain, 2007*)

www. Elizabeth Kubler-Ross Kübler-Ross model; Stages of grief in terminal illness; The stages, popularly known by the acronym DABDA

www.ushistory.org/civ/4g.asp Promise of land and fulfilment verses.

Wikipedia: The terms *anno Domini*[note 1][1][2] (AD) and before Christ[note 2][3][4][5] (BC) are used to label or number years in the Julian and Gregorian calendars.

https://www.birdforum.net Bill Oddie quote '17 sept 2007

http://www.beliefnet.com/prayers/christian/death/love-is-stronger-than-death.aspx#uuSSRmSSxKwVrMzg.99

www.goodreads.com Mother Teresa Quote

Steinhauser et al 2008; Questions from Australia- Preparation and life completion intervention questions

Film 'The Inn of the Sixth Happiness' about Gladys Aylward a maid who felt called by God in go to China, (Twentieth Century Fox, A CinemaScope Picture, 1957)

John Kennett, Song, Faith Can move Mountains (2008) from the CD 'Held in the Fathers Hands' by John Kennett & friends.

Don Moen, Song, God Will Make a Way (1997)

Revd Nick Fawcett: The Teacher, A Simple Guide to Daily Life, (Kevin Mayhew, Croydon ,2016)

Rainbow Bridge – Author Unknown